CHINA
IN
FIVE
CITIES

KERRY
BROWN

Published by
ACA Publishing Ltd.
University House
11-13 Lower Grosvenor Place,
London SW1W 0EX, UK
Tel: +44 20 3289 3885
E-mail: info@alaincharlesasia.com
Web: www.alaincharlesasia.com

Beijing Office
Tel: +86 (0)10 8472 1250

Author: Kerry Brown

Published by ACA Publishing Ltd in association with China Translation &
Publishing House

Hardback ISBN: 978-1-83890-015-1
Paperback ISBN: 978-1-83890-011-3
eBook ISBN: 978-1-83890-012-0

A catalogue record for *China in Five Cities: From Hohhot to Hong Kong* is available
from the National Bibliographic Service of the British Library.

经典中国国际出版工程
China Classics International

CHINA IN FIVE CITIES

FROM HOHHOT TO HONG KONG

KERRY BROWN

ACA PUBLISHING LTD

CONTENTS

INTRODUCTION

I was born in the county of Kent in the southeastern part of the UK in the late 1960s. Kent is rich in history, a crossing point between the ports of Dover and Folkestone on the coast and the northern parts of the island, via the city of London after it was established in Roman times two thousand years ago. Kent is small (less than 4,000 square kilometres, a mere five times larger than Shanghai's municipal area) and existed as its own kingdom till the eighth century. It was then amalgamated into larger kingdoms. Its identity, though, has always been strong. And it has perhaps of all the British areas the richest literary history. Geoffrey Chaucer, one of the first great English-language poets from the fourteenth century, often came here as part of his work as a government official (collecting taxes and spying). Charles Dickens, one of Britain's greatest novelists, spent much of his childhood here in the early nineteenth century and lived in the western part of the county as an adult till his death in 1870. Ian Fleming, creator of the James Bond 007 spy novels, had a house in Kent and wrote some of his thrillers while staying. The poet TS Eliot sat in a beach hut by the sea in Margate in 1921 and pondered his future after a mental breakdown, writing parts of his seminal poem 'The Wasteland'. HG Wells, author of the world-famous *The War of the Worlds*, lived in Folkestone, a town on the southern coast, and the great director Derek Jarman owned a house and small but extraordinary garden in Dungeness. Perhaps most extraordinary of all was the Ukrainian-born Polish sailor Joseph Conrad, who made the villages around Canterbury his home in the latter part of his life. It was here, writing in his third language, that he produced *Heart of Darkness*, one of the greatest twentieth-century novellas, which he set on a ship moored near the port town of Gravesend. Kent was even the home of the wartime leader and winner of the Nobel Prize for Literature, Winston Churchill.

I was educated at schools in Kent, in the state system – first at a primary school and then a grammar school. And through them, I gained a position at Cambridge University and read philosophy, then English literature. My interests were, throughout this time, within the Western tradition. Greek philosophy, English thinkers like Locke and Hobbes, and Europeans like Wittgenstein and Kant – these were the staples of this kind of education: English empiricism, with continental idealism regarded as an exotic counter-tradition. This was a world that began and ended with the Western canon, and where the ability to read and think in French or German was regarded as unusual, and acquaintance with Russian language and literature 'oriental' and exotic.

Later on, I became acquainted with arguments by figures like Edward Said, the American Palestinian writer, describing the tradition of Europe as self-absorbed, and criticising the way in which it confined everything outside of this cultural sphere to that vast area called generically and unhelpfully 'The Orient'. As a schoolboy, and at university, places covered by this vast term seemed not only to be unknown, but unknowable. My earliest memory of anything Chinese was the face of the then Chinese leader Mao Zedong on television in September 1976 when his death was announced. A decade later, I acquired a large history of Chinese civilisation by French scholar Jacques Gernet, and tried to read it. But it seemed to refer to a timeline and a narrative of history that I found impossible to relate to the European ones I was familiar with. In that tradition, lists of the reigns of kings and queens of European states and different emperors and empresses gave me a backbone by which to have a handle on the progression of history. But Chinese imperial dynasties were complex and went back deeper into the past. Their names were so unfamiliar, and histories about them seemed to refer to a sense of time, and a story, wholly different from that of Europe, and one where, apart from occasional contact during the Yuan Dynasty in the thirteenth and fourteenth centuries and the modern period, events paralleled each other but were not remotely interconnected.

In my school library, the only book relating to China was an Everyman edition of Confucius's *Analects*. But a reading of that when I was about fifteen was bewildering. With no metaphysics, and no straightforward argument such as I could find in the almost contemporaneous *Republic* of Plato, the book seemed to be a collection of cryptic utterances. On television, China was a subject only sporadically glimpsed: some documentaries, and occasional mentions in the news of the reforms under Deng Xiaoping, which were then under-way. But apart from this, China was remote, behind its famous Great Wall, an object I was told (wholly incorrectly, as everyone knows now) that was visible from the Moon.

People of Chinese ethnicity in the UK were largely at that time those who had either come to the UK as migrants, or who were the children, or descendants, of earlier arrivals, largely from Hong Kong or Guangdong. There were China-towns in cities like London and Manchester, and Chinese restaurants – but again, these were exotic places, and the food that they offered, I found out later, heavily adapted to British tastes. For all of that, they were some of the few places where I could see Chinese characters – mysterious swirling figures utterly unlike the Roman alphabet – or Chinese art, on scrolls or watercolour pictures, and with a style completely different from most Western art I was familiar with. There were very few students of Chinese or Asian ethnic heritage in any of the schools I went to. Indeed, the first person of Chinese ethnicity of my age I actually talked to in any depth was a student at Cambridge from Singapore. The simple fact was that in the 1980s and even the 1990s, Chinese tourists and students in the UK hardly existed.

My first encounter with Chinese writing was reading 'The Cantos' by the American poet Ezra Pound. Pound, through the early twentieth-century scholar of Asian cultures (partic-ularly those of Japan) Ernest Fenollosa, had become acquainted with some Tang and Song poetry in translation, and, without fully understanding the meaning of the charac-ters, had incorporated them into later sections of his epic poem. They sat on the page, between the other lines he had written in English, or Italian, French or Latin, mysterious, stark, and almost disconnected from the text around them. Pound included transliterations, in the old Wade Giles system, in his text and translations to explain the characters he used – and he also devoted a whole section of a poetic account of the rise and fall of some of the Chinese dynasties. But the effect, in this poem, rendered in this way, was to reinforce the sense that China and Chinese language, history and culture was radically different – so different as to be almost unknowable. China, I could conclude from this, was difficult and complex.

Making Chinese knowable, and accessible, happened to me personally by accident, rather than intention. I was not a good linguist. My French was passable after two months spent in Paris at the age of 18, and I was, and still can, read it relatively well. My German after two years was almost non-existent, and attempts to self-study Latin and Greek got hardly anywhere. If I had presented myself to a university in 1986 as a potential student of Mandarin Chinese, I would never have been accepted. Chinese was consigned to the 'most difficult' category of languages. That meant only those with proven skills in learning languages could get on formal courses to study it. Oriental studies at Cambridge was a mysterious, very niche area – I met one student in my whole time there on this course. It seemed highly technical, and those pursuing it almost invisible. That reinforced the message I had from before that this was a subject for only the most hardcore, serious-minded scholars. China and Chinese studies were for the elite of the elites, people with a deep vocation – it often seemed almost like an exclusive religious cult.

One of the books I had been most impressed by around the mid-1980s was *Auto-da-Fé* by the Nobel Prize for Literature winner in 1981, Elias Canetti. The central figure in that, Peter Klein, epitomised the stereotype of a sinologist. Based in Vienna before and during the takeover by the Nazi Party in the 1930s, Klein lived a life of severe self-discipline and pure devotion to his scholarship. The book starts with a dialogue between him and a young boy in which he explains the meaning of a Chinese character. But as the story develops, his life complicates and darkens. He enters into a disastrous marriage with the only person he has had any regular contact with over the previous few years, his housekeeper. She proves to be a grasping, greedy and brutal person. The other figure who appears in his life is a sinister dwarf, and his whole story escalates out of control, resulting in his final demise and the ruination of his orderly, controlled life.

Auto-da-Fé is a work of wonderful originality and strange power. Often written in an almost semi-hallucinatory style, the choice of career for the fictional Klein is puzzling. Why of all things did Canetti decide on him being a sinologist, rather than a classicist, or a scientist, or an expert in literature. Part of the reason must be because this area above all others confers a degree of otherness on him, and grants him a kind of mystique. The same might be said of the use of Chinese characters in Pound's work. Neither had any deep understanding of Chinese language or, for that matter, any lived experience of China. The one poet from the West who did live in the country for any length of time over this period, William Empson, produced works that, tellingly, were devoid of any extensive mentions of the country where he spent over a decade in the 1930s and 1940s. Perhaps familiarity to him cured him of any temptation to 'exoticise' China. Even so, despite being a hugely accomplished intellectual, it seems he did not study or learn much spoken Chinese while he was there.

Klein was a poor role model for a career that I was one

day to end up pursuing. Until the end of my university life, therefore, the best one could say was that the British educational system I had been through, excellent and comprehensive in so many ways, had given me only the most patchy and superficial knowledge of the culture, history and language of a fifth of humanity. In some ways, it was worse than this. I had also been exposed to hardly anything about Asia more generally. That situation became increasingly anomalous as I grew older, and is one of the puzzles that I often think about the cure for today. How was it possible to be highly educated, and yet not educated in some key areas at all?

CP Snow, a scientist and academic, had complained in the 1960s about the problem of the 'two cultures' – that of the worlds of natural science and physics or biology, and that of literature and the humanities. His critique was savagely lampooned by the critic FR Leavis in the early 1970s. For Leavis, there was only one culture, and different modalities of it – which science, humanities and other thought forms were parts of.[1] But I could say that my educational upbringing had made me aware of a similar kind of 'two cultures' – ones which seemed almost segregated from each other, those of the West, and of the East. How could this great divide be remedied? That is the key theme of the stories in this book.

———

Up until 1978, one could argue that there were many reasons why China, in particular, was less known about. In the age before instantaneous electronic communication and easy mass plane travel, for one very practical reason – physical distance – China and the UK were very remote and often inaccessible to each other.[2] Then there was the issue of cool political links between the two up to the 1970s, when there wasn't even a full embassy in each other's capitals – only legations. All of that was removed by the rapprochement between the US and China in 1972, which meant the UK was able to upgrade its relations with the People's Republic, giving it ambassadorial status the same year. Finally, there was largely a lack of real commercial engagement. China was a developing country, a small economy, and one that was, till the 1980s, largely dependent on primary industries and agriculture. It simply didn't have the kind of logistical and people-to-people links with the outside world that meant it was present in the lives of those in other countries in ways which, for instance, the US or Australia were. Added to all of this were language problems. The UK and China did not speak the same language. And very few people from either place, even without the above-mentioned impediments of distance and lack of direct links, could have communicated with each other even if they were physically able to meet and link up.

All of that has changed in the second decade of the twenty-first century. There are 110,000 Chinese students in the UK in 2018. China is an investor and trader with the UK, and the rest of Europe, and the world, in ways that were not the case before 1978. In 2017, 120 million Chinese tourists travelled abroad. That figure is likely to increase by 20 million a year from now on. Chinese signage is now on shop fronts, greeting people at airports, appearing on adverts on their mobile phones in even the most hidden-away parts of Europe. If you live in the West, you no longer need to search China out once you develop an interest in the country and its cultures and history; it will, no doubt, come and find you.

And yet despite this transformed situation, I suspect that children and young people can still go through the educational system in the US, Europe or elsewhere and come out with as patchy and incomplete a knowledge as I did three decades ago.

It was a sheer accident that I eventually came to invest the time and effort into understanding China, and to learning its language. There was nothing planned about it. A teacher at university had spent time in Suzhou and recommended going to China to look – but I did nothing about this till I worked in Japan in 1990 for a year, and took the opportunity to fly the short journey from Osaka to Shanghai and Beijing in May 1991, during the famous Japanese Golden Week holiday. Being a tourist in Beijing at this time with not a word of Mandarin was tough. The hotel I stayed at, City Hotel (now no longer), was near Sanlitun and the Workers' Stadium. I was too afraid to use the underground, even though only two lines existed at the time, and I could only go to restaurants where the menu was in English. Every day, I walked the two miles or more, often in very hot weather, to the Friendship Store, and then on to the Beijing Hotel. I made one attempt to see the Great Wall, by going to what was then a small train station in the south of the city and showing the ticket seller a sign for 'wall' (*qiang*). Needless to say, she had no idea what I was trying to ask for. On this occasion, at least, I never got to see the great sight.

I did at least by this time know some written Chinese. I had been studying *kanji*, the loan characters from Chinese in the Japanese language, in the town of Nagahama, central Japan, and had managed to memorise about five hundred. Many of those, however, were in traditional, rather than simplified form, meaning probably about half were recognisable when I tried to interpret menus and other signs in Beijing.[3] The week I spent there was a challenging experience. But it also created a kind of bond. The place seemed both very different, and yet very familiar, in ways that were wholly unexpected. The idea of China being 'unknowable' and profoundly mysterious and beyond comprehension started to be seriously challenged. This was a place full of humans like in the world I had come from, trying to live their lives, and going about their business in ways very similar to that of my home town. A six-month stay in Melbourne, Australia after I left Japan in 1991 reinforced the idea that China and the Chinese language were things I could and should be more knowledgeable about.

Despite its distance, Melbourne was a good place to try to at least get a start on learning Chinese. It had, for one thing, an excellent book shop with learning material in the China-town in the heart of the city. And China seemed far more present here than it did back in London. There were more Chinese restaurants, more people of Chinese ethnicity, and, most important of all, some non-ethnically Chinese who had mastered Putonghua ('standard speech', the phrase referring to Mandarin) – and therefore made it clear to me that this was something one could do even if it wasn't an inherent part of one's cultural and family background. The greatest inspiration came from a person I was lodging with at the time – Andrew Beale, a native Australian, but someone who had mastered the language of China to fluency, and who taught it at a secondary school. Days and weeks speaking to him about his life and experiences in China had a huge influence. I am glad to say he is still a good friend to this day, almost thirty years later.

Making China knowable was important. Every day, I

would try to memorise a few more Chinese characters. I was working in a duty-free shop specifically catering for Japanese tourists, of whom there were plenty at this time. They tended to come in large groups, entering and leaving the premises, and making large, unbusy gaps in between. I would stroll around the shop, with a pad in my hand, convincing the manager I was occupied doing inventory and stock checks, but actually writing down all the characters I knew. Usually I got to about seven or eight hundred. I even kept a primitive diary in Chinese. I tried to learn Chinese at night, and during the journey in and out of the city centre on the tram. The problem was, however, that while I could work out the grammar well enough (and be overjoyed by how much more familiar it seemed than gender-infested German or declension-drenched Latin), even coming out with the simplest spoken sentence often proved impossible.

Back in the UK, I found that there was only one practical, year-long postgraduate diploma course in Mandarin Chinese. It was here that I hit the issue of how specialised and exclusive studying Chinese was in the British system again. Leeds and the School of Oriental and Africa Studies (SOAS) both did masters courses, but with very limited language learning. The response to most of the places I spoke to was that I either learned Chinese privately (which was extremely expensive) or did a whole new undergraduate degree, taking up four years. Only a place called Thames Valley University, which had gone under the name Ealing Polytechnic before these more vocationally orientated institutions were upgraded, had something affordable, and practical. Even then, without a bursary from the Great Britain China Centre I would have found it hard to embark on a degree.

My memory of learning Chinese in earnest therefore is

not of living in Beijing, or Shanghai, or some of the places mentioned in this book. It is instead of sitting in a small bedsit in west London, near to Acton Town tube, over 1993 and into 1994, and learning passages, reading Chinese novels and newspapers with a dictionary by my side, and having conversation exchange partnerships with about half a dozen people, sometimes putting in ten hours of study a day. For eight months I did this, trying almost to create a little world of China around me in a city thousands of miles from the country I was becoming so interested in. If I bought books, they were about China. If I went to films, they were the few then being shown which were in Chinese. I tried to eat each day in Chinese restaurants, and get whatever knowledge I could about China. When I went to second hand bookshops I would trawl through the bookshelves trying to find anything relevant – some of it over a century old – that related to China.

This could almost be called my second education. I started to know that there were figures like Cao Xueqin, author of the great Qing Dynasty novel *Dream of the Red Mansion* (also known as *The Story of the Stone*) and historic figures like Sima Qian, the Grand Historian from the Han Dynasty almost two thousand years ago. I came to appreciate that Confucius was one of a large number of thinkers around the Warring States period, four centuries before the time of Christ – living, writing and thinking alongside people like Mencius and Han Fei and Mo Zi. For the first time I learned of Lu Xun, the greatest of the early twentieth-century Chinese writers, and of events like the May Fourth Movement in 1919, and the anti-Japanese war from 1937. I read Edgar Snow's *Red Star Over China*, the first account in English of the rise of communism in China and then his subsequent visits to the country in the 1960s. I learned about oracle bones, the First Emperor, the Tang Dynasty, and the voyages of Admiral Zheng He in the early fifteenth century. It seemed an extraordinary thing that this world, which was there all the time, had never appeared to me. But then, like most other people in the West, I hadn't been inclined to look, and had been given the impression that even were I to seek, what I would find would prove too difficult to understand. Carl Jung, the psychologist, and one of the Western intellectual figures of the twentieth century most interested in Asian religion, philosophy and belief systems, had categorised humans as 'symbol loving species'. I guess one could add to that that humans are, through symbols, lovers of stories. One of the great challenges of engaging with China was to try to create my own understanding of the China story I needed to construct, and what my own version of this would be. Chinese history was long and impossibly complex. But it was also, at first inspection, full of contradictions – a country that was new and old; one that seemed diverse and yet uniform; a place where for much of its history there had been no unifying framework supplied by adherence to a common belief system, as had, eventually, happened in the West from the fourth century onwards through adoption of Christianity. There was this China of what looked like industrialised cities and the other place which seemed to have jungles and pandas still living in the wild there. This place was not an easy one to fit into any preconceived box. It seemed to evade easy assumptions and frameworks. And Chinese people, after all, during the early period of learning about the country, were not that present even in a major centre like London to allow me direct experience and contact to correct misconceptions.

The only remedy for that was to actually go and live in

China. So I applied to work for an organisation partly funded by British government aid money at the time, Voluntary Service Overseas (VSO). That was the reason why I spent two years in the Inner Mongolia region of China from 1994, where, to all intents and purposes, I finally managed to speak and read Chinese with some fluency – and, after a fashion (as the first chapter will show), write it.

———

The 'unknowability' of China, and the need to move beyond that and make not only a China story, but one that is honest, truthful and, above all, manageable, is the main theme of this book. The personal account I have given above at least offers some context for why someone who had never had any link whatsoever with China came, from their mid-twenties, to increasingly focus on the ideas, history, literature and people of this geography. Since 1994, I have worked as a diplomat, business person, consultant, and then finally academic, for most of that time in, with and on China. I have been to every single province and autonomous region, lived in the country for over five and a half years, and visited more than a hundred times. From 2006, I have written twenty books on China, lectured about the politics, economics and history of the place in over forty countries in four continents. I have lived over three years in Australia, working as an academic dealing with China, and back in the UK. Over that period, I have been interviewed by every major news outlet, from CNN to BBC to Sky to ABC and Al Jazeera, along with what was once China Central Television (CCTV) and is now China Global Television Network (CGTN). I have written on China for the *New York Times*, the *Telegraph*, the British *Independent* and *Guardian*, the *South China Morning Post, China Daily*, and about every other major European-language newspaper or internet journal. If anyone would have told me even in 1989 that I would have a career like this, I would have regarded them as crazy. At most, I thought I would specialise in English literature. And until 1989, I wanted to simply stay in Cambridge and continue my career there. If I had a dream, it was an English one, not a Chinese one. This book is primarily, therefore, a story of how that England Dream became the China Dream for me.

Before anything else, I have to say that entering and then living this 'second life' has, whatever its challenges, been a source of great joy. And if anyone reading this who is in the same position I was thirty years ago is encouraged to make China and its rich culture and literature knowable the same way to themselves that I tried to, then that would be reward enough for writing it. Sharing the pleasure of knowing about China, and coming to know China better and deeper, is the principal meaning of my professional and much of my personal life now. Seeing that there was another realm, a different world with a different view of life and destiny, was immensely liberating. And while there were periods over the era of this encounter in my life when things were very challenging – when it seemed extremely tough to fit in in China, and hard to make sense of many of the things I was experiencing and seeing there – that has all been immeasurably outweighed by the returns of investing in understanding the country and getting to know some of its people better. China being knowable for someone who knew woefully little about the place till quite late in their life is my main theme. And showing the many different strands of that knowability, and the ways in which it can be shared and understood by almost everyone else who devotes some time and effort to it, is hugely important.

The way I have chosen to convey this in this book, however, is distinctive. A simple autobiographical account would have been tempting but in the end too limited and subjective. It would be one narrative amongst all the others of those who weave in and out of the life of China, or who belong to the current country's great and vast national story. My objective here is to aim for something that might be a little more useful, and give some ideas or tips about just how those unfamiliar or new to China might make what they see and experience there part of this mission to make all aspects of the country 'knowable' without losing the integrity of its 'otherness' and difference. This is not a popular idea in the post-Said era, where Orientalism and creating 'otherness' is regarded as discriminatory and limiting. Despite that, I will try to show in this book that there is a point beyond this where one can see the familiar and the unfamiliar in one organic, balanced, embracing vision, and hold them with their uniqueness while also seeing what connects. The great work of divination from the earliest dynasties of China, the *I Ching*, talks of everything being connected. Striving to under-stand and appreciate those points of connectivity, but also see clearly where margins, boundaries and division lines are, is important.

In fact, this lay behind the work of someone I did, very peripherally, know about, and physically at least see a few times, from my college days. The Cambridge college I spent three years as an undergraduate at, Gonville and Caius, was the home of the great scientist and scholar Joseph Needham. He was, in the time I was there, in his mid to late 80s, a stooped, venerable-looking figure who would slowly pass across the quads on his way from his rooms to college dinner some evenings. I never managed to speak to him, but was alerted to his great work, *Science and Civilisation*, and to some of his long and distinguished experience of China from the 1940s. I had, too, at least one thing in common with him: he had clearly come to studying and understanding China relatively late in his career, after an early period where he had been a biochemist. Needham had worked at the British Legation in Chongqing as a Science and Technology attaché in the latter part of the Second Sino-Japanese War period, when the nationalists moved to this southwestern city, then in Sichuan province, to make it their national capital in the early to mid-1940s. It was there that he had been alerted to the rich history of scientific thinking in China, dating back to the pre-Qin period, and to the eras in which China had historically been an innovative and inventing powerhouse. This inspired the rest of his life – resulting in the many volumes of his great work, some authored by him, some by other experts, which continues to this day. A few years after I graduated in 1989, he died, aged 95, in 1995. One of his obituaries noted that he was the greatest European scholar since Erasmus, of the early renaissance period.

Needham had answered one of the enquiries about what had drawn him to China so deeply by stating that engagement with the country and its intellectual history and the values underpinning this had been an exposure to something wholly different from that of the Western tradition he had been born and brought up in. It offered an alternative, another way of looking at reality. When I deployed this line at a talk in Shanghai sometime in the mid-2000s, someone in the audience rightly pointed out that this was 'orientalist'. But even so, it seemed to me an idea I was reluctant to give up. China didn't exist on another planet, for sure. But it had a clearly different set of social practices, a narrative of its histories, and a whole attitude towards the world that certainly differed from the tradition I had grown up in. How could I ignore that?

In this book, I have decided to focus on something tangible, and very physical, as a way of telling my China story, but also illustrating this issue of difference, and how differences can aid the quest to make something more defined and knowable. Place is something that always fascinated, and continues to fascinate, me in my life in England – the relationship of particular places, for instance, with the lives of writers, something I mentioned at the start of this introduction, in Kent. The memory traces, as they are called, that are left after major events in places like fields where battles occurred, or buildings where major events happened, or cities or towns that testify to the many different kinds of lives that have been lived there over the generations. Ancient places were of specific interest – fragments of old churches in the UK that went back to the earliest period when Christianity was being spread here, in the fifth and sixth centuries, or the faint traces of roads from the Roman period that are often left in the landscape, or domestic buildings that, despite modernised facades facing the high streets, were clearly very ancient behind these, or woods that had Iron Age or other remains covered up by shrubs or trees, but still were just about visible.

Coming to a new city, right from when I was quite young, I would always try to get a map of it in my head. This was helped in Britain, and Europe, by the simple fact that almost every place, however old or new, usually had a specific pattern – a church or churches, or a cathedral, somewhere near the centre, and then perhaps a city or town or village square, with businesses, restaurants, a pub, hotels, and, spanning out from this, parks, monuments, major streets, leading to other hubs and major features. Sometimes there were very visible public buildings – government offices, or institutions, or museums. At other times there were art galleries, or newly rebuilt areas where the feel and features of the buildings were wholly different. All of this helped build up an idea of age, character, and contributed to the sense of place.

One of the great challenges in exploring places in China, as this book will illustrate, is that the layout and geography, and the meaning of particular places, along with the best way to interpret these, are very different. Contemporary China, the place I have been visiting and familiar with over the last quarter of a century, is somewhere that has undergone, and continues to undergo, immense physical transformation. Cities can change in the space of a few years, so they are often almost unrecognisable from the first time one visited. This only adds to the original problem – how someone from a different cultural background can start to 'read' the terrain they are physically walking in when it is so changeable. Temples instead of churches is one of the easier issues to readapt to and be alert about. But the ways in which city space and town space is organised and managed, the functions of buildings, their style, the ways in which you can date them – all of this needs different kinds of knowledge.

For someone non-Chinese like me, navigating and coming to terms with a new place in the country is challenging. But it is absolutely necessary. One issue is the very practical one of climate – of how because of temperature, it is frequently not easy to walk far in Chinese cities, particularly in the southern more tropical areas, where being outside for only a few minutes can leave you drenched in sweat. The other is how often paths and roads in China are not easy to walk along – simply because there is so much traffic, and so much of it is different (bikes, vans, lorries). Chinese cities, unsurprisingly, are far more crowded than most Western ones because the population is greater. Their signage is different, road etiquette completely unlike the UK (crossing roads in China can be famously challenging, rules of the road are different, and the status of pedestrians also different). Very finally, in many Chinese cities, particularly further back in the past, when I walked around I was conspicuous, the only person with fairer hair. It was hard to simply fit into the crowd. If I stopped to look at something, I sometimes gathered a crowd of onlookers around me. In recent years, with the rise of foreign tourist numbers in China, this issue has become almost negligible.

What sense one makes of what one sees, however, is another matter. Local histories, and the ways in which places testify to events in the past, is largely conveyed through very general guidebooks, and then in Chinese language material, which is, of course, harder to access. The places I have written about in this book are mostly well studied and well known. There are many other books about them, many in English. Even so, getting real intimacy with their stories is not easy. So this account is predominantly personal – and not a pretence at writing anything like an authoritative history or account of these places. In that sense, it simply offers a history of me understanding and growing to have feelings and impressions and attitudes towards these different cities. It is a history of the meaning of these places to me.

The places I have covered all have symbolic importance to

me. Hohhot, in Inner Mongolia, was the city I went to in 1994 to work for VSO at the Inner Mongolia Medical College. Whatever I knew about China, I knew next to nothing about the climate, location, culture and history of this place. For two years, I studied Chinese there, in the main local university, while teaching postgraduate doctors English. I went back many times after I departed in 1996, and saw the physical transformation of this place. But this is also about the grasslands, stretched around the city, and the difficulties of trying to understand their geography and atmosphere.

The second chapter covers my experience of the capital, Beijing, from my first visit there in 1991, to the period in which I lived there from 2000 to 2003 as a diplomat, and the times I have been since. In some senses, as Beijing is the place I best know in China, this chapter operates more as a palimpsest, offering up different parts of the city and different times when I visited. The best I can do is to choose some of the most meaningful places, and create a personal narrative from this.

The third chapter is of a place I have actually written a whole book about – the great city of Shanghai. This is in some ways the account of a conversion – from disliking the city because of its sheer size and energy when I first visited in 1998 as a freshly appointed diplomat still based in the UK, to spending a great deal of time in the city at the end of the next decade, working on the link it had with Liverpool. It was over this period that I grew to appreciate the extraordinary atmosphere of the city and the way in which it so dramatically conveys some of the contradictions, and the innovations, of modern China.

The fourth chapter is about Xi'an, the great Tang Dynasty capital, and home most famously today of the Terracotta

Warriors. I visited this city for the first time in 2000, taking a British official delegation there, and then returned to it many times, becoming increasingly fascinated by the almost endless residue of former dynasties and previous Chinas in the buildings and historic artefacts left in the city. This section tries to deal with how one can make that immense history with its complexities and differences knowable when one comes from outside of it, and the ways the physical layout of Xi'an and the residues left in the landscape with their epic, fragmentary nature can help with this.

The final chapter is on Hong Kong, only restored to Chinese sovereignty in 1997, but a place that maintains a unique atmosphere, and which has proved perhaps the most difficult to make sense of. My Hong Kong is not that of a long-term expatriate there, but of someone who has enjoyed many short visits since my first encounter in 1991. For me, therefore, Hong Kong is a special but very Chinese city – an international Chinese city, perhaps, and one that has physically changed the least of those in this book, but offers examples of transformation in other ways. It is also a place that, as a British person, I have a distinctive emotion towards.

There is a final strand that runs through this book, and the places I have listed above. That is the business of understanding that most mysterious thing of all – everyday life. When I worked at the British Foreign Office in the late 1990s, I remember one day a colleague I was working with sighing and saying that he had 'no idea what most people fill their time with'. In fact, it is even more perplexing than that. We in our own lives, the lives we live, which we alone have complete ownership over and scrutiny of, often have little idea of where time goes, and, when gifted with the freedom and ability to deal with our time, are often overwhelmed or unable to structure it well. We keep busy, we bury ourselves in distraction, and find targets, ideas, things to chase after each day. Sometimes, too, we cede control over the majority of the waking hours we are conscious in by subscribing to the structure and discipline of whoever we work for. In London, most people commute, get on trains, sleep, read the paper, wait till they arrive at their terminus, then get onto buses, or other means of transport, and then go into the place where they work. Most of the time, these are offices, more often than not communal ones, meaning one deals with a specific circle of people each day, with the pleasures, reassurances and challenges that involves. There are meetings, lunches, appointments, times before the computer, times on the phone, times in meetings. The grammar of daily life in post-modern societies, for all the variety, is often standardised, no matter where one lives. For me, even in the times when I lived a life like this (thankfully, not very often) it was always a case of trying to create more variety, more stimulation, more engagement in the prescribed daily structure that was supplied for me. Probably many people are like this – creative about the opportunities open to them, making the structure of the day more bespoke. But there are limits. And bosses are often intolerant of too much creativity in this area.

The structure of my day and of everyday life in a new place, as the following separate accounts of the places will show, was often different. In Hohhot, I was immersed in a new cultural and social context and from day one had to find coordinates, familiarity and reliable routines, things that shaped my time. I had limited teaching hours – the rest was for me to fill. And as someone wholly fresh to this place, that meant challenges, creativity, a sense of being on an adventure where there was freedom to do things and shape things and a great deal of self-determination. But there was also the task of learning new social norms, new codes of etiquette, new boundaries that I had to be heedful of in order to integrate and settle in. We all know of the intolerant outsider, the person who comes, particularly from a Western context, into a place like China, and expects, wants, demands things to be absolutely as they had found them back home. The constant battle to achieve what is impossible, because of course things cannot be the same, often leads to a period of fractious battle with the environment and the people in it, and then either reconciliation and adaptation, or, more often, dissatisfaction and departure.

In Beijing, I was working for an organisation and lived a more structured life. In Xi'an and Shanghai, and to some extent Hong Kong, things were different. For these places, I was a visitor, never staying for more than a few days at any single time, passing through, and had limited commitments to and a circumscribed engagement with the environment I lived in. That entailed a certain amount of privilege – not needing to grow too attached to the place, able to exercise the detachment of an observer rather than someone too implicated and owned by a place. But the range, and depth, of feelings for the second kind of relationship to a place are very different from the first. That will hopefully come across in my accounts.

This interest in the basic structure of everyday life gives the accounts that follow a different kind of flavour. These are not travelogues. They are not accounts of seeking the exotic and strange, nor are they trying to use the privilege of an outside perspective to tease some deep 'message' from each of the places, and put them into some kind of objective narrative of what China is, how it has to be seen, what its meaning as a country or a culture is. Instead, I have recognised the subjectivity of what I am conveying. There was me, with my set of experiences before I arrived at a particular place, the background I have described above, and the interests I had – and then there are the illuminations that happened when that life, that set of experiences and expectations, happened to then be placed in the new environments mentioned in this book. In a totally different context, the Anglo Saxon historian Nicholas Howe wrote in his book on looking at ancient sites in the UK from the period of the Dark Ages about how this involved negotiating two realities – the site seen, and the seer, the person looking, with their sets of knowledge and ideas. Visiting Bede's World, a modern museum commemorating the work of Britain's earliest native historian from the eighth century, Howe writes that he needed to balance two times, and marvelled 'that a place could hold in suspension two radically different moments in British history separated by twelve hundred years – agricultural village and industrial landscape'.[4] In China, for me as an individual, as will be seen, this became a constant preoccupation, particularly as I started to know enough to critique my knowledge and understanding of what I was seeing and experiencing, and to see it in a richer and more complex context.

The French philosopher Michel de Certeau wrote in *The Practice of Everyday Life* a rich set of observations about what constituted this 'mysterious thing' – the business of simply going through each day as an individual. Daily life to him is not the most common and normal thing, but something loaded with different symbols, the site, in fact the only site, where meaning is created, and where goals and stories and aims are defined. Daily life is the ultimate space, the place where life itself happens, not something humdrum and

demotic and boring. One of the ideas he articulates is that of
frontiers between different spaces of our daily lives – that of
work, of leisure, or rest time and active time, intimate time
and active time – all of these of course circumscribed by the
cultures and habits and modes of behaviour of the larger
environment within which a single individual's life is
inevitably embedded. In that sense, a daily life can be seen as
a rendition like a soloist of a larger 'text' – the sorts of expectations, beliefs, desires and ideas that arise in any society and
culture and which everyday life is an iteration of.[5]

It is not often that one sees lives from such different
cultural backgrounds properly described. A lot of material,
much of it very good in terms of its honesty and complexity,
is written in English, French, and other languages describing
China and life in China, the life of Chinese, from the point of
view of an observer. The privileged position of the authors of
these kinds of works is based on their linguistic distance,
their specialist knowledge, and their desire to demonstrate
neutrality. David Bonavia, one of the finest earliest journalists
from Europe working in China after reforms started in 1978,
produced, soon after his time there, an account simply called
The Chinese.[6] No one could contest his knowledge of the environment he lived in. He was a superlative linguist, and a fine
journalist. But there is distance built into his account, something that is true of all similar endeavours produced since. It
is as though someone were looking through a telescope and
seeking, and finding, in an object wholly separate from them,
differences, and not only differences but differences that are
evidently meant to mean something, and to imply an almost
irreconcilable distance.

In this account, I have simply tried to cure this problem of
distance by focussing on the things that would unite people,

whatever place and background they came from – the physical environment they have to exist in to be people and be in a place with its smells, sights, sounds, tastes, and the ways in which these construct narratives and meanings – and the simple temporal existence of people each day, living in time, patterning their daily habits, no matter whether they are Chinese or from elsewhere. Chinese time as I experienced it in the different places described in this book was something I lived in, as a perpetual outsider, but it of course changed and forced adaptation on me. I had to observe the sort of customs of time boundaries in each place I found myself in – the times of shops opening and closing, the moments of the year when there were major festivals, the habits of people each day when they had siestas, or ate, or were watching television, and it was best to either join them in adopting these habits or refrain from contacting them till a suitable time came up. The space that China is, and the time that it has as a place, are present as threads throughout this book, and transcend, it seems to me, the issues of culture and habit. They act as fields in which things and people can actually do the business of living. That, in essence, is my theme – the way in which I, coming from elsewhere, negotiated, adapted and changed the places and times of the locations in this book. A simple subject, for sure, but one that is so utterly essential, and so often ignored, as a means of describing how finally a bridge can exist between two such different worlds and traditions and cultures and histories of China, and of the West.

HOHHOT

浩呼
特和

The material I had been sent on a few A4-sized typed pages with some hard-to-decipher photocopied black-and-white images was unpromising. I had applied to the VSO organisation mentioned in the Introduction and gone through a series of interviews and aptitude tests in London. I had even attended a course on preparing for how to live in other cultures in a centre near Birmingham. But the day on which I finally found out where I was to go was unsettling. I wasn't even sure if Inner Mongolia was a place where standard Mandarin was spoken much, which was my whole reason for going to live and work in China in this way in the first place. I needed an environment where I was exposed to the language I wanted to learn twenty-four hours a day – otherwise, I might just as well stay in London and continue to learn with people I could do language exchange with here. But the few pages of information on what, I was told in the pack, was called the 'blue city' because of the colour of the skies, was unambiguous: this was a place where standard Chinese was spoken widely. I would be fine.

Arriving in Hohhot in early autumn on the overnight train from Beijing meant navigating a whole set of new sounds, smells, and experiences. The first impression was chaotic – a typical station, before a typical town, full of people coming and going, carrying vast amounts of luggage. I had been in soft sleeper the whole way – a version of the first class on some British trains, with relatively comfortable bunk beds, and only four people to the cabin. Getting out meant appreciating just how many other people had been travelling with me on the same train. But it was also disconcerting going through the night with the steady sound of the vehicle, most of the time moving, but often stopping at stations, occasionally sounding its horn before it slowly started shuffling off again. We had travelled into darkness, and so I wasn't able to see the outside world until I arrived, at dawn. But even on the crowded platform, disembarking, the air felt thinner and colder than in hotter, muggier, more humid Beijing.

That first night, the only place I got to see was the college that was to be my home for the next two years – Inner Mongolia Medical College, founded in 1956 when many from elsewhere in China had settled in this region bordering the Republic of Mongolia to its north. The college lay along a central, long, straight street called Xinhua Road – New China, the words to commemorate the founding of the People's Republic in 1949. The inside of the college was divided into three parts: the main teaching building; the hospital affiliated with the college; and the living areas, a series of apartments that must have been erected in the 1950s to the 1970s. Interspersed with these were some smaller single-storey structures where bikes and vegetables and other belongings were kept.

Over the next few days, I got to know more about this

microcosm. It was a very typical 'work unit' (*danwei*), a complete world within a world – with its own businesses, schools and medical and welfare facilities. My apartment was one reserved for foreign experts – the college had been hosting these since the 1980s. A simple one-bedroom second-floor flat with a living room, a vast, ancient television, a fridge, a black PVC sofa and a bookcase. In between there was a bathroom, and a kitchen in a narrow space. The only other facility was a tiny balcony looking across to the facing buildings.

What sense did I make of this new environment? Britain didn't have work units, for a start. These were the principal form of social organisation, at least in urban China, from the 1950s. But even by 1990, with Reform and Opening Up, things were changing, and plenty of people had lives outside of the places where they happened to be physically accommodated. In the mid-1990s, too, many people were buying their homes, and renovating them. A neighbour one evening told me enthusiastically about the new business opportunities that were starting to appear everywhere. Some of this was already evident in the shops that were dotted in the courtyards around my home. Most were privately owned, or managed in an arrangement with the college. At night, they always impressed me because they never seemed to close, and they always had tremendously colourful displays – piles of fruit and vegetables for sale, or stock of biscuits and imported or branded locally made goods, under an array of bright lights. The same went for the restaurants, most run as small affairs by entrepreneurial managers, and vying with each other for business. This even worked on the level of tradespeople coming into the small lanes between the housing, calling out for people to buy things, have their kitchen knives sharpened, or their bikes repaired.

Once within the space reserved for the college, things were more formal. The main buildings there were the library, the teaching block at the centre, and the administrative offices. All were in brown to grey stone. Over one side were dormitories for students. The conditions in this college were quite basic – eight to a room, with communal cooking and showering facilities. There was also a large canteen, and a smaller one which I used a few times at the beginning for visitors, until I started to cook my own food. Classrooms were bare, with rows of desks – and the occasional map or portrait on the whitewashed walls.

Through a small door along a wall at the northern side of the college living area there was a backstreet, running between two major roads. That was the limits of my exploration of the environs of the college in my early days. It led down to a wet market, a street full of stalls, with meat, piles of vegetables, dry goods, preserves – a place perpetually full of people, even till late in the day. For me, used to British supermarkets with everything neatly labelled, and the almost zero interaction with members of serving staff, this was completely alien. Going to one place for meat, one for sugar, another for bananas, and having to haggle over the prices I paid for them sometimes was hard. So too was pointing at a sheep or cow carcass hung up on hooks, with its flesh exposed, and seeing the butcher carve off bits of meat and weigh them on hand scales.

Early on in my time in Hohhot, a chef undertook to teach me how to cook food in a properly Chinese way. One of the earliest dishes was 'twice cooked pork'. The night before the lesson, he came around with a list of ingredients. My first task was to come to this market and find pork, oil, ginger, soy sauce and onions. Back in the small kitchen, with the one wok on its gas hob, he poured in the pork, fried it, added ginger, poured in some soy sauce, and then sprinkled some onions into the mix, and within minutes the food was on my plate with rice he had boiled. The next time we did pork fried and covered in batter – *gan za zhu pai*. But the dish I really acquired a taste for was one I discovered in one of the tiny eateries off by the side of the market – *yu xiang rou si* ('fish strands of pork' in the literal translation, though there was no actual fish in the meal itself), something in a soya sauce base with carrots, strands of meat, and spices. That became the staple for me for much of my time in the city – and remains something I'll always eat with a Proustian sense of memory of the place where I first discovered and devoured it.

You could walk through the market with your eyes closed and smell the different foods. In that sense, too, it was different from Western supermarkets. The smells were sharper, more vivid, and more various. Out on the main street, it being later in the year, the trees lined their way up to the main city square. This was the second place I managed to wander to, trying to carefully expand my world. People's Square was the heart of the city, or at least its largest heart, because I learned later that one of the characteristics of Hohhot was that it was a city with several centres, despite the uniformity that seemed to have been imposed on it during redevelopment. On one of the bright sunny days over August and into September, the square was stark – paving slabs with a fountain that sometimes played in the centre. At the southern end, looking down there was a series of large boards with Chinese characters written across them, celebrating National Day, which was about to happen in a few weeks' time when I first visited. Over on the east side was a large bookshop, taking up several storeys – one where I found a remarkable set of every major novel by a winner of the Nobel Prize for Literature from the first award to the 1980s. North was the tallest building in the city at that time, the tower of Inner Mongolia Television, and, next to it, the only hotel that claimed four stars and international standards – the Zhaojun Hotel.

I would sit in the lobby coffee shop of the Zhaojun Hotel some nights, in the early weeks – making sense of the new city, looking at the murals on the wall there. The story of Zhaojun was a celebrated local one – a Han princess who had, two thousand years before, married one of the Inner Asian tribal chieftains from the Xiongnu. But this was all part of that vast and intimidating historical narrative I was only starting to understand the barest outlines of. One afternoon, I went to the bookstore and managed to get a wall chart of Chinese emperors. The line was often divided, and the names no easier to remember, largely because it was clear they had several – given names, imperial names, honorific titles. In the Zhaojun, too, there were restaurants that served Western food (or, at least, some burgers and pasta), Chinese food (which seemed to mean Cantonese and Beijing duck) and then 'local delicacies'. That meant Mongolian lamb – mutton, sometimes boiled on the bone, or roasted, and then laid on communal tables for guests to eat.

———

Sometime in the early weeks in Hohhot, the Foreign Affairs office for the whole city decided to arrange a holiday for all the experts, to go out of the city and see some of the grasslands. I'd been told about this before even arriving in Hohhot – the location of the place, the way it existed on a plateau of rising ground, leading to mountains and then beyond that the vast flat areas of grass where sheep and other livestock were raised. From within the city, it wasn't easy to imagine what the surrounding country was like. Some days you could see the mountains to the north, a soft, pastel blue. But you had to travel quite a way out of town to start to imagine the countryside around. The one attempt I made at the start on my 'Flying Pigeon' standard-issue bike didn't go well. Two punctures, and I had to come back, finding the road too hard, and the traffic too heavy. The tour was with a coach, though. So that should mean I really got somewhere.

What did I learn on that first trip? That there were other foreigners, non-Chinese, in the city, most from America, one from Canada, and that some had been here for almost a decade. That travelling beyond urban areas meant you had to adopt a different sense of time in China – at least in those days. You would just aim to arrive in the afternoon, or the morning, and make no commitment beyond that. At one point, the coach simply rode through the faintest of trails in what looked like a mixture of sand and grass. For some reason, we reached a telegraph pole with wires where the driver had to delicately navigate through, something that took almost an hour. Often, roads simply ended and we had to go along a dirt track, negotiating our way with smaller vehicles or other lorries and cars passing by. The nights were spectacularly dark.

During the nights, too, getting out of the coach wherever we had arrived, the sky was staggering – stars clear, their light falling down upon us. There simply was no light apart from that of the coach front. When we got to the destination, a small, border town called Xilinghaote, it almost happened upon us, rather than making any announcement. One moment, we were on an open road seemingly in the middle of nowhere, the next we were in amongst low, dark buildings, one of the slightly taller ones being a hotel. When we did manage as a group to wander around the town centre, all we could find were small shop kiosks still open – and the occasional well-lit tiny bar. In the morning, the town seemed even smaller – a few busy streets, and then the grasslands almost as soon as we left them.

I had no expectations about what we would see, but I do remember the most powerful impression was made at the end of one of the middle days, when we had been coaching for most of the afternoon. We stopped off at what we were told was a commune, and got plied with lamb, rice cooked in lamb juices, and then some white spirit – a kind of very powerful local brand. After clambering aboard the bus and starting a singing competition, we were stopping before some shallow mountains and what looked like two mounds in the foreground, though they had an explanatory board in front of them. The information on this was in Chinese – a simple text, with the name of what we started to appreciate was a significant monument before us. Someone deciphered the heading – *Shang Yuan Du. Shang* was the character for 'up, on top'; *Yuan* that of the Mongolian dynasty between the 13th and 14th centuries; *Du* was capital. After pondering it for a while, someone provided the solution: 'Xanadu,' they said, triumphantly. That made sense. The semi-mythical place had been spoken of by Western poets like Samuel Taylor Coleridge from the great Romantic era in England, whose brief, overpoweringly evocative piece 'In Xanadu' had immortalised the place.

Coleridge's work was very familiar to me. In my final year at college I had written an extended essay on him, going to the British Library to inspect the manuscripts deposited there which he had written. One in particular, a book on logic, had been important to me, largely because many of its ideas, critics claimed, were taken from the sources of others without proper acknowledgement. Coleridge was a problematic figure – an idealist and revolutionary who had become, in later life, staunchly conservative; a drug addict; a great poet who had largely fallen silent in his middle years, before producing a late flurry of work to match his great early period, working in collaboration with William Wordsworth when young. Coleridge above all had been a key figure in introducing continental enlightenment figures like Kant and Schelling to the English-speaking world.

The writing of 'In Xanadu' had itself become a myth – the story of a poet in an isolated house, overwhelmed while taking drugs, by inspiration, and writing fluently lines that he intended to be the start of a longer work. Coleridge, however, according to the standard story, had been interrupted by a tax collector, and once they had gone, so too had his poetic mood. The poem therefore was an all-too-brief delicious fragment. In many ways, this served as the metaphor for his life – someone intensely productive into his twenties, and then suddenly unable to produce anything for years, blocked and inhibited, until finally the muse revisited him.

Coleridge had never visited China. He had never in fact been further than Malta, where he served, unhappily, as an official for a few years in his middle age. But most scholars agreed that his knowledge of the eastern ancient city had come from Marco Polo's travels in the thirteenth century and its description of the summer palace of the Yuan Dynasty emperor Kublai Khan, and a massive, half realistic, half fantasy work from a century before him, the 'Pilgrimage' of William Purchas. That too I had dug out in the antique and rare books reading room of Cambridge University Library one afternoon before coming out to China, and tried to read through its closely printed pages.

The real site of Xanadu could not have been more surprising. It was as though someone had laid a thick, green fluffy cloak over the eroded ruins of what were once buildings, streets and architectural features. Here and there, standing on the shallow mounds that marked what must have once been the entrance gate, there were sharp features – promontories, small outcrops, and the occasional shallow gulley and cavern. Sporadically, around the edge of the abandoned city, there were remnants of earth walls. Marco Polo, coming here eight centuries before, had been profoundly impressed by the summer capital, celebrating its luxuriousness and splendour, and the ways in which different animals were kept as pets in the city. But after the fall of the Yuan in 1367, the capital simply shifted first to Nanjing, and then back to Beijing. The new imperial rulers did not share the nomadic, mobile habits of their predecessors. Xanadu had in effect been derelict ever since.

There was little there, and yet it was a hard place to leave. Even persistent calls from the coach driver didn't shift me from my observation point until someone came to collect me and accompany me back on the bus. The atmosphere of the place was what made it so special – silent, with light failing, dusk coming on, and this place of such great cultural influence and fame dwindling once more for another night of darkness, and visual oblivion. Clearly very few tourists ever came here – even from other parts of China. But it had a haunting quality, and one that remained with me even after I finished in Hohhot and came back, in 1996, to the UK. Rifling through a bookshop one day soon after my return, I found a whole book on the place, by a British woman, Caroline Alexander, who had visited some years before me.[1] Others had clearly made it there, some even cycling, despite it being in what was then a prohibited military area around the city of Jining. I didn't ever think I would have another chance to get back there though, and the city slept as much in my memory as it evidently did in the landscape it was enclosed by.

A few years later, however, while working as a diplomat in Beijing, I had dinner with some Italian and British friends. One of them mentioned their visits to the city of 'Shang Yang Du' and how they were working on a plan to make the place a new 'eco city'. It seemed a bold and surprising idea. They had often travelled there by car on the weekends – it was a seven-hour drive – and they believed the place had great prospects because of its proximity to Beijing, and its name recognition factor. They had even set up a website, with some idealised drawings and mock-ups of what a reconstructed Xanadu might look like.

Their plans, however sincere, didn't seem to have materialised by the second time I managed to get to see the place, in around 2007. A decade or more on from my first encounter, I realised that the site was in a township called Zhenlan ('True Blue', in recognition of the colour of the sky most of the time here), and that there was a small cluster of buildings nearby. By this time, I was working as a consultant, trying to nurture trade and cooperation in China with foreign, and particularly European, parties. The idea had occurred to me through a friend to see if the local officials were interested in promoting Xanadu, now in a non-restricted area, as a tourist destination. After all, it had a certain evocative appeal – a few days in Beijing, for visitors, capped off by a night in yurts close to the old Yuan Dynasty capital.

The idea seemed a popular one. Someone else in Beijing became even more ambitious, suggesting that a hotel chain like Shangri-La be encouraged to consider opening a five-star property close by there to accommodate people. There might be helicopter landing pads for those wanting to come from Beijing more quickly, or a luxury limousine car service from Beijing, because the motorway quality was far better than even a few years before. In the end, though, the location remained much as I had first seen it – a mysterious stretch of land with the tiniest suggestion of its former glory, surrounded by empty grassland. In many ways, this was more appropriate. Visiting Xanadu had, and continues to have, an almost dreamlike quality, a place to let the imagination wander and to pick your way between the few standing structures and the undulating, uneven ground.[2]

If there was one way to really enter the spirit of this city, and of the grasslands themselves, then that was to sit cross legged in one of the yurts in the evening, eating, and listening to performers singing the remarkable 'Khoomei' two-toned throat singing songs. Well delivered, this music is captivating – a single singer able to produce from their throat a high and a low note at the same time. The music seemed to weave and play around in the air, suggestive, evidently very ancient, and conjuring up much of the haunting emptiness of the great landscape all around us.

———

The epic qualities of that landscape were the thing that started to intimate itself to me on the first visit – but which came back with even more force as I became a little more knowledgeable about the geography Hohhot was located in. Clearly, travellers from Beijing by train, and particularly those by car or plane, could sense how the land rose higher, and how Hohhot was on a higher altitude than the capital. But even the eleven-hour journey between the two I had taken only made up a tiny part of the extent of the autonomous region. From Hohhot, you could go on a regular bus to the other main industrialised city of Baotou, three hours to the west. That was spread out over three centres, and was best known for being where a vast iron and steel plant was based. Around Christmas 1994, I took the bus ride to spend time with two other English teachers living in the college there – a journey where I wore far too little and went down with a terrible cold. But Baotou was only a small step into the vast terrain that lay before Amen, the most westerly part of the region, where, reportedly, the richest and most extensive grasslands were. I didn't see more of that than what was visible when I travelled by train from Urumqi in Xinjiang back via Yinchuan to Hohhot in 1995.

Even this two-day journey just intimated at the sheer scale of what I was looking at. And it made me appreciate that for all the fame of China's huge population, there were spaces in the country that were emptier than any in the UK.

Hohhot's formal part, that at the centre, spread before the train station and the People's Square, were my first world. But there were parts of the city, almost other cities in their own right, that lay beyond this, and which I started to appreciate as I became more adventurous. One of the most remarkable was in the old city, along a wide road immediately south of my college. Either side of the road here, in amongst narrow backstreets and small sidings, were two temples. One, from the Qing Dynasty, was made of wood – with a series of shops just outside its gate selling tomb masonry – tall steles ready for Chinese characters to be inscribed on them, or shorter gravestones, a little like those one saw in memorial parks in the west. The temple itself was calm, usually empty, a place to sit before it grew too cold, and meditate. But I did not understand the kind of services that the monks, sometimes passing by in yellow or dark brown robes, undertook. Some days when I went there, there would be chanting. On others, there would be the sounding of a bell.

The temple on the other side of the road was larger – three courtyards as one went in, through doorways into spaces where even bigger buildings reared up. The final one had statues of large Buddhas, draped in silk scarves, with offerings before them. It was the artwork on the walls I liked about this place – mandalas, patterns showing heaven and hell, placed on the wall. One day as I came out, I saw an elderly lady with tiny bound feet. She must have been by then in her late eighties or early nineties. She stood almost precariously, before the gate, in dark clothes, her faced lined, and I wondered when I looked at her what things she must have seen in her life – the end of the final imperial dynasty, the Qing, before it collapsed between 1911 and 1912; the Republican era, when the warlords divided China up and saw the country slowly move to war, attacked by the Japanese from 1932. The Japanese indeed had come to Hohhot during the war from 1937. She must have known the period of occupation, and the Civil War from 1946 that followed it, along with all that happened afterwards. Here she was, standing in a city that was, even in the mid-1990s, in the midst of further change. I wondered what sort of home she went back to, how her family looked after her, what kind of life she was living now. But she disappeared quite quickly, walking with a speed that surprised me. Foot binding had probably ended when she was no more than five or six. She must have been one of the last people to have undergone the ordeal.

The old city went according to a pace, and had an atmosphere that was different from elsewhere. The buildings were mostly made of wood and some brickwork, usually no more than two storeys, most of them around the temples selling incense, a smell that drifted out on late afternoons and prepared you for going into the temple precincts. There were miniature statues of the Buddha, and, most intriguingly of all, piles of fake money to burn for those who thought this gave them good fortune. I knew how to interpret and read churches in the West because of long familiarity with them, and understanding of the rituals of Christianity particularly on the Catholic side. Even the smallest church in Britain was like a meeting place, but one laden with symbolic meaning – somewhere people would try to reconnect with what they believed to be the divine. Churches were full of images of Christ and the saints, with particular fittings that recalled his life and resurrection. Even the shape of most churches – a long body with two side arms – recalled the body of Jesus, laid out as though to be crucified, the sanctuary his head, the nave his body and the transepts his arms. But the space of temples, the meaning of particular parts of their fittings, the many, many different kinds of figures and statues – these were all unfamiliar to me. And I didn't understand properly the kinds of services held here. Were they like Christian services, usually conducted on Sundays, but sometimes during the week, where there was a set liturgy, or the kinds of burial and marriage or baptism ceremonies most churches convened in the West? They certainly seemed mysterious places, their courtyards tremendously still, with a few trees providing shade, and stone benches on which to sit. But the meaning of these places as buildings did not make much sense to me back then. They were largely historical structures, a reminder that the city I was living in had existed for several hundreds of years.

The old city of course had shops – small kiosks around the mosque, for instance, which stood with its minaret at the edge of the district, Islamic signs around the precincts, and, when prayers were taking place and I went by some days, men and young boys in distinct white robes and headgear disappearing into the prayer hall. Here where the food needed to be halal, signs said that the meat had been ritually prepared. There were even carts with large bags of raisins, dried fruits, and spices which smelt as pungent as the incense in other parts of the city. Old men and women, evidently from the countryside, sat either by the horses tethered to the carts, and on small stools, sometimes chewing sunflower seeds, watching passively as people walked by. Some of them had wares laid out on sheets on the floor – selling sunglasses, clothing, books, or small electronic gadgets. Others were even selling small pets. That was the thing that was common across the city, I thought – the constant presence of trade, either through shops, stalls, or peddlers.

This was a merchant's city, a place for selling things.

New buildings were being built all the time, even on the edges of the old city. Some were vast new restaurants, catering for the newly emerging business people who were grasping the economic opportunities opening up because of reform. Others were blocks of flats, sold off to those who were now working mostly in the ever-expanding private sector. One day, a friend took me to the new flat his father had just bought. It had the standard shape of most of the structures being put up then – a large living room, kitchen and shower room at the back, and then two, sometimes even three, bedrooms. These places were usually plain on the outside, and then, when you came through the door, immaculately clean – ceramic tiles on the walls, ornate wooden furniture, and, in this house at least, a large new freezer and television. A dog was barking somewhere outside – pets were legal but you needed permits. Despite the cost, most people seemed to want to own a dog or cat. One of the pictures on the wall was very familiar to me – a small church by a bridge in the area of the UK that I was from, a distinctive blue-faced clock telling the time on the church tower face, and old buildings crowded around it. Looking at this scene so far from home made me momentarily nostalgic. Since I had come here, people had often asked me whether I missed home. At first, I could sincerely say I didn't. But looking at the peace of the place like that portrayed in the small painting brought back memories of often going around these buildings, learning about them, walking through them, and trying to understand their history. In many ways, that was what I was doing in this new temporary home – trying through acquaintance to create an emotional bond with a place where so much needed to be learned before one could really feel anything except confusion.

The city did have parks. The largest of them, the People's Park, was in the more commercial district. It had a large entrance and then immediately before it an artificial lake. In the good weather, people would paddle across this on small plastic peddle boats, most of them made in the shape of ducks or swans with the heads of these animals at the prow. There were restaurants, coffee shops, small businesses adjoining the lake, and then beyond this space for small paths between trees. There were no roses or flowers of the kind you got in the carefully planned gardens of the UK – but plenty of green leaves, shoots, and stems, and at the back a small menagerie. You could see from within the space of the park the first of the modest skyscrapers starting to appear. Of course, years later they would be more numerous, taller, and more imposing. Just up from the park was the main commercial street. When I arrived, the main shop was the Nationality Store, the closest to a department store in the West. Opposite this, in a city which in the mid-1990s had yet to acquire any of the fast food chains like Kentucky Fried Chicken or McDonald's, there was the closest thing Hohhot had – a place selling fried chicken and ice cream. I sat there often in the early weeks, seeing the occasional tourist trudge in and out, wondering what had made them choose to come to such an isolated place. They were no doubt wondering the same thing about me.

Moving to a new place involves not just adjusting to the physical environment, but also creating a pattern in your daily life as soon as you can. Routine helps to defray anxiety and feelings of homesickness and isolation. At least you are starting to control your own time and put it to use. Almost as soon as I moved into the small foreign experts' apartment, I realised that the college and the community around me had their own particular daily patterns. College terms saw different things happen. Out of those, like in every other university on the planet, students would disappear, and new people arrive. During term time, a tannoy sounded up every morning, and then once it had finished there would be stirring music. Sometimes, one could hear the roar of soldiers practising in the central square – all students back then had to do military drills, so perhaps it was them. Then there were the calls in the morning of peddlers coming around in the alleys between the houses to sell things. The same thing happened in the evening. That was when I learned to go down with an empty litre-sized plastic bottle and get milk from an old Mongolian man on a bike who carried two large containers that he pulled the milk from. Before drinking, I had to boil this. His call was unique – *Da niunai lai le!* (Milk is here!) Even now, I can remember the way he shouted this and how I had to listen carefully at a particular time each evening in case I missed him. One time he even had a severe cold and so could barely rasp, but I still managed to catch him. Milk was, is, important!

The rest of the day was patterned around two things – work and eating. Work was partly teaching for the college. That, though, was not onerous. The postgraduate group were small – about twenty people. They were all training to be doctors to be sent out to various parts of the region. They needed English for professional interaction with the rest of the world and for the ability to read specialist journals for their work. For them, I did one lecture each week, and then two seminars. For the wider community, I would do a public lecture. The rest of the time, I was left to my own devices. And in that, I read, studied Chinese, and tried to educate myself about where I was.

The slabs of time for study were interrupted by lunch and then dinner. Hohhot seemed to fall still when lunchtime came. Even the traffic appeared to stop. It was a mass ritual.

When people in the flats around me came back to their homes, you could hear the cooking utensils moving, the gas hobs being fired up, and the clatter of woks and pans on metal surfaces. After this, silence reigned. Most people napped for a while. It was a peaceful time of the day, and made me realise that for all the drama and mystery imputed to the lives of others like the Chinese, who were seen as different to Westerners, in fact at heart their lives were built around daily rituals like this – eating, resting, then going to do whatever work they did.

Dinner was more active – restaurants nearby filling up, the more popular ones overspilling into the street. Around September into October, it started to become too cold to eat outside. But until then, in my very early months, you could see in People's Square vendors selling small kebabs, grilled fish, tiny snacks – it seemed each stall had its speciality. The most fascinating evening activity was the mobile karaoke machines, where young people would belt out their favourite songs, and, depending on where you stood, you could hear fragments of their voices drift across the square. Just to the north of the square, nestled at the back of the television station building, there was a more formal singing place – a small Beijing Opera theatre, with a restaurant attached to it. The clue to the function of the place were two tell-tale painted masks at the entrance. Inside, the main part of the building was a theatre, with a small proscenium arch, where ornately garbed performers walked out and sung some of the best-known, distinctive, Beijing Opera classics. You could wonder as you watched them how they acquired this skill, when in their lives they had become interested in being performers, and what sort of training they had gone through. Out back, just behind the stage, you could spy other performers waiting nervously for their time to go on. The audience ate their food, occasionally applauded, at other times were busy with their conversations, barely heeding what was happening before them. But the atmosphere was relaxed. No one seemed to mind.

Back out in the street, until the coldest part of winter, you could still hear the karaoke singers roaring out their words. They followed you on your way home to the college. And at times, I could even hear them back in my flat. Once the cold came, though, Hohhot was a transformed city. At the coldest point of the year, in January and February, it dipped to minus twenty-five, sometimes even minus thirty. But this was not a straightforward coldness. It bit at you when you went outside, seemingly benign at first, and then penetrating almost through to the bone, like a sharp-toothed dog. Dry and persistent, the cold spread everywhere. Even the smallest puddle of water on the street was permanently frozen while the winter months went on. The lake in the park became a skating rink. Because of the opportunities to practise, the locals were so good at this they were able to send people on behalf of the national team to participate in the Winter Olympics. One lady promised to teach me how to skate – but I proved too clumsy and unable to maintain my balance unless I had something to hold on to for her to give me more than a couple of tries.

The city had a number of different universities. The main one, Inner Mongolia University, had been founded quite soon after the creation of the autonomous region in 1947. It had an impressive front space before a main building with a tower rising up over administrative buildings, and lecture halls beside it. I came to discover that this was the standard set-up for an educational building across China. I came over here from the first month every Thursday morning after I arrived, to have a couple of hours of Chinese teaching with a professor in the Chinese language and literature department. She introduced me to figures like the Tianjin writer Sun Li, and two of the country's greatest modern writers – Yang Jiang and her husband Qian Zhongshu. It was a laboured process, however, to go through their writings, checking almost every character in my Oxford Chinese-English dictionary, making its pages stained and grimy because of the number of times I thumbed through it. Some characters, usually the most simple, because of the lack of an easily identifiable radical (the standard part of most characters used to categorise them), used to take me hours to track down. The teacher suggested I get a reverse dictionary too, because most Chinese 'words' are a combination of two characters, and often I knew the second but not the first. On top of this, I had a dictionary of proper names – the transliteration of translation into Chinese of figures like Beethoven, Mahler, or Dickens. The final piece of my linguistic armoury was a *chengyu* dictionary – a list of four-character sayings, some of which came from ancient folk wisdom and memory within the spoken and written language. When I had done this, the Chinese teacher would listen to me try to read the pieces of literature I had selected each week, making sure I came at least a little close to getting their tones right.[3] After that, we would discuss what we had just read and she would give some background. She was an excellent teacher – patient, knowledgeable, incredibly effective. I am still grateful to her decades later for the help she gave me.

Just down from this main university there were a series of more specialised ones – the teachers' university in the southern part of the city, which was a little further towards the suburbs, and then the agricultural college for those who would go into farming and rural management. There was the industrial university, a little to the north, and, further still to the northwest, the Mongolian Vocational College, the only one that used Mongolian language as the primary means of teaching. All of these universities and colleges had people interested in and engaged with learning English. And all of them operated as small worlds of their own, with their rhythm of life and communities and set of mini cultures. I knew this because the foreign teachers I had become acquainted with there told me about the slight differences between my life in the medical college, and theirs. The main issue was that I was teaching students who were much older – frequently in their late twenties, or early thirties. One or two were even coming close to forty. Most had married. Many had already had children. Some had even travelled abroad. Their perspective on life was very different from undergraduate students, who were usually around twenty, and had almost all the major decisions of their life to make.

The college area had one characteristic I grew to appreciate during my period of wandering – small, narrow streets, bunched in all directions around it, with tea shops, tiny bars, and cramped, miniature shops. Most striking for anyone who visited for the first time were the pool tables along the side of the roads. These were run as businesses, with one person sometimes renting out two, three, or even more tables for games. The green velvet of the tabletops was covered over in tarpaulin when it was too cold, or on the rare occasions when it rained. But almost all the rest of the time they were open to the elements, with people playing on them. This in itself was a remarkable sight – players with great force smacking balls from one end of the table to the other, trying to get the red or blue spotted ones in depending on which they had first of all elected to sink. I had no talent at this, even when I played it from time to time in the UK. I would hold the cue, chalk its tip like I knew what I was doing, then lower myself, line up the white ball and the target, and proceed to smash it with no direction or control, usually seeing it going in a completely different direction to the one I wanted, as though it had a will of its own. I rarely potted anything except by mistake or good fortune. In Hohhot, it was little better. Friends who invited me to play on the roadside were patient and gracious. There was no expectation that anyone would do particularly well, and the main thing was just to show some spirit and play. Most other people seemed to have the same level of technical ability as me – creating huge thumping noises as the balls collided with each other, but leaving the same number on the table despite interminable attempts to sink them. Games seemed to go on forever. They had a sense of great leisure and timelessness. I sometimes wondered when I waited my turn to play if the afterlife would be a sleepy eternity of playing a game of pool like this that just went on with no resolution.

Those who did happily somehow terminate a game could then head into one of the tea shops nearby. There were literally dozens, perhaps hundreds of these – and every single one was different.

Proprietors expressed their individuality in a myriad of ways. Some hung Western-style posters on the walls. Others went for a more severe, ascetic look. There were lurid colours decorating the interior of some, and gentle pastel colours for others. Neon lights had been contorted into extraordinary shapes so that they could create patterns on the nearest surface. Often these made what looked like characters or words. At night, this was particularly effective, creating a street scene that was vibrant and lively. These tiny places seemed to be screaming and competing with each other for attention. But when I went there, they were rarely very busy – and they were almost always open, even early in the morning or late at night. Tea too was not the tea I was used to – it often came in bowls, and it was milky, made of brick-shaped tea, which was boiled in enormous kettles, poured out steaming and usually kept boiling perpetually on a stone or overexposed flames. These were refuges for peace, comfort, distraction, in the end, rather than places where one would come to drink for its own sake. The tea was salty – I never saw anyone commit the abomination of adding sugar, which is so often the practice in the UK. And they often added small beans of corn which were bullet hard at first, and then softened in the liquid so they became a little more edible, after a while floating on the surface creating what looked like a skin. The other snacks were boiled or roasted peanuts, small bowls of Mongolian sweetbreads, biscuit textured, but again more salty than sweet, and delicately moulded Mongolian cheeses. The common element here was that everything was made of sheep products – sheep milk, sheep fat, sheep cheese. If there was one thing that was unique about the smell of Hohhot compared with most other Chinese cities, it was this ubiquity of the different odours of sheep. Boiled mutton, the aroma of roasting joints of lamb, the general scent of sheep and sheep products was every-where. This was a sign of the sheer prominence of sheep for the region's economy, from ancient times right up to the present. For centuries – probably millennia – sheep had been grazed on the vast grasslands around the city, which I had briefly visited. If a blind person had been taken to the city, they would have been able to tell immediately that this was a place where sheep were important, and were a staple part of the diet, their skins and furs worn, and their presence felt almost everywhere. Not that I saw many live sheep within the built-up areas. At most, there were occasional sightings of one or two being led by a shepherd coming into town to do something. But they were more a subliminal presence, known by the products made from them, not by their physically being present as live animals.

Tea shop street and bar street morphed from one to the other, and some of the tea shops served as both cafés and pubs, depending on the time of day. On Friday nights and into the weekend, the areas around the universities, as they did throughout the rest of the world, became turbulent with students out to have some fun, either singing or drinking, and socialising with each other. Some groups started to belt out songs together, while others were engaged in earnest conversations in small huddled groups. In the winter when it was extremely cold, ducking into one of these places because of the warmth and the ambience became akin to seeking refuge from arctic, inhospitable iciness in a minuscule, welcoming oasis of warmth and light. In the night, they shone resplendent, their facades and windows with stickers advertising their special deals and cooked food, blazing visions with darkness all around. I could sit here, usually untroubled, getting on with some reading or writing, or just musing, while life went on around me, alone and yet in company.

Hohhot never, in my time there, saw snow. But it did have the most impenetrably foggy days, partly through pollution (smogs at night were sometimes relentless), and partly through the cold. When the cold came, the city changed its appearance, and so did its people. In the non-human world, trees became bare. Buildings looked even starker in the winter light. Because of the relative lack of cloud cover and the bright sun, the quality of that light was always special in Hohhot – unblinking and fierce to the eye, particularly on blank, pale surfaces, and the cause of the dryness that was a feature of the city. For people though, the impact was even greater. Everyone went around shrouded in layers of clothing. Life moved inside. The vendors still appeared outside, but largely under many different layers of fabric, with thick leather boots on their feet. Even the facial area had to be covered up. When the cold came, riding a bike became particularly treacherous, patches of ice felling even the most skilled cyclist. I became adept at slowly balancing myself on my bike, looking a little like a circus performer as I wobbled along the side of the road, going wherever I was going. You often saw people collapse in an undignified heap if they hit a spot of slippery ice they had failed to see. It happened to me many times. The only consolation was that the thick layers of clothing insulated and protected the flesh underneath. Wounds were rare. Torn clothing was common.

The inside life of Hohhot over these winter months was spent in restaurants, people's homes, which were heated by stoves or central heating. At a particular time of the year, the heating came on. The cold indoors vanished. The radiators that delivered this warmth were remarkably effective. Coming in from outside was like going from extreme to extreme – from the Arctic to the Tropics. I could sit in my room and think the world around was basking in lambent warmth. But looking to the apartments opposite mine, I could see the cabbages and other vegetables stored on balconies outside, and be reminded that the external world had, indeed, become a vast fridge. In this icy terrain, the white spirit, the rice wine so many locals loved drinking, started to come into its own – warming up the body of whoever drank it, cheering them up, before, of course, the next day, when the hangover took away all the joy that had been created. With friends I had acquired in the city, however, sitting in small restaurants and talking, laughing, singing during these months, made me realise that in a way, Hohhot was now coming, for all its initial difference, to seem like it was indeed a second home.

———

The physical city I have described was one that I guess every visitor, however short or long their stay, had to adapt to their needs. For me, from my first weeks there, I built up a place I could be comfortable with – finding out where I might be able to buy certain foodstuffs, where I could get cooking oil, where I might be able to buy tape cassettes (they were still in existence then) or go into small parlours to watch performances of video films, the latest blockbusters imported from the West. Finding restaurants where the food was good, or tea shops that suited me, were all tasks I soon sorted out. But on top of this was the business of searching, and sometimes finding, more specialist requirements. Sometimes this was just by happy accident. One day I was passing by a row of shops and noticed the cartoon of a baker holding out cakes. When I went in, I found they served what looked like chocolate gateau with cream on them. When I tried them, they tasted OK, with no nasty surprises like a salty or savoury flavour. Further visits showed that this shop sold good quality bread – quite crispy and nice, evidently freshly baked. That was a huge and happy discovery. The other luxury was Western-style chocolate, on sale, for some reason, in the shop at the Zhaojun Hotel, but quite expensive because it was imported from a factory in Australia. This became a weekly treat for me after I had discovered it.

Sometimes I learned about things I needed simply by word of mouth. Foreigners living in the city were a source of information for each other. One of them heard of a factory in the local city of Baotou that produced decent quality cheddar cheese. It seemed unbelievable. But a friend visiting from that town one day brought a large slab, and it tasted authentic. It even had the same pungent smell and crumbly texture. That slab lasted for a few weeks, carefully wrapped in foil and conserved in the fridge the college had supplied me with. Another find was brands of Western-style food products – tins of fruit and jam, for instance, and even the occasional rare supply of home-produced biscuits or snacks. Most days, though, if I cooked, I did so with the simple implements I had been given – a two-ring gas hob, a saucepan and a wok. The two staples I manage to find quite quickly were frozen packs of lamb dumplings – which took about ten minutes to prepare – and instant noodles, produced by a Taiwanese company and very popular in almost every shop I visited.

My life in the new city came to take its own shape and direction. But I was always aware while I was there that I was simply passing through – and that after two years from the day I arrived, I would head off, either back to the UK or to some other place. To me, the physical shape of the city, the different atmospheres that existed in its constituent parts, the ways in which I tried to make sense of it, presented themselves as a puzzle I had two years to work out the solution to. I formed a distinct circle of friends and created my own network within this city. It was, in effect, my city while I lived there – a customised copy of the original one, with its own routes, and paths and areas I liked to visit. But there was this perennial doubt I had that I was never really able to work out what sort of place I was living in, and that much of its life and reality either remained hidden or unknowable to me. It would be fanciful to speak of the philosopher Immanuel Kant's distinction, at the height of the Enlightenment in Europe, of there being things as we perceive them, and things in themselves (phenomena and noumena were the terms he used for these differences). But that, in effect, was what I experienced – the city as a palimpsest of sensations, spectacles, and visual or auditory or olfactory impressions, which I had created through my experience there – and the city that really existed. I was always trying to come to grips with it and get to understand it better. In that second place, reality always seemed to be just out of grasp – either over a wall I was walking by but couldn't find an egress through to get to the other side, or at the end of a street I was walking along but didn't seem to be able to reach, or just over the brow of a hill I was climbing up.

That was made powerfully clear to me one day when I was standing by the newly built Tianyuan store, a sign of changing things with its vast interior, and its newness and prominence, showing that local Chinese people were able to afford far more than ever before, and wanted more choice and better quality goods. It was a weekday, and there was no reason why I should have expected anything unusual. But Chinese New Year had just passed, and that went on for a week or more, with different parts of the festival on different days, after the main day, the one that marked the start of the Lunar New Year.

Down the main road before the shop, a huge procession made its way towards me – parading people dressed in festive garb, some on stilts, made up like the mythical figures in the great *Journey to the West* epic novel of the Ming Dynasty. This had told of the scholar monk Xuanzang's great tours in the Tang Dynasty, around the seventh century, and his heroic battle over almost three decades to bring Buddhist scriptures and practices into China. The novel was often televised, a sort of amazing fantasy full of mythical beasts and magical happenings. It made up one of the five great novels in the Chinese language, alongside *The Story of the Stone*, *The Golden Lotus*, *The Water Margin* and *The Romance of the Three Kingdoms*. Seeing people made up as Sun Wukong, or Monkey as he was popularly called, the main figure in the story, was extraordinary. But here, in daylight, was a fantastic display of acrobatics, people in fancy dress, a riot of colour, carnivalesque in its vibrancy, with figures marching by me playing flutes, banging drums, and calling out to each other in between the music. The procession seemed to go on forever, made up of discreet different groups of figures, some male, some female, some wholly fantastical. After what seemed an age, they receded into the distance.

I had no idea about who might be organising and taking part in this parade, or observing it. But they stretched before me, each of them carrying their own unique stories and their own lives in the city that I was temporarily living in. Maybe some were like me, just passing through – here to visit relatives, or working away from home. What I did realise was the richness of life in this place, life that I was barely able to scratch the surface of – the pace of life that people in the old city lived, the life that people in the colleges and universities were passing, the life of those in the thousands of small and large shops, in the hotels, and the various businesses, and of those working in the government, or the local officialdom, or as teachers, doctors, other public figures. The city was a vast jigsaw puzzle, and much of that puzzle was aptly symbolised by the parade that went before me that day.

In 1996, in the summer, during one of the most comfortable times of year, I left Hohhot after two years of studying and teaching there. The usual parties were held; the college said goodbye to me – some of the friends I had made and others showed a huge amount of hospitality. Hohhot had truly changed my life, in ways that the year in Japan when I was slightly younger had not, because it had not touched me at the most personal level. Even months after leaving Hohhot, back in Britain, I remembered the terrible cold winters, and the way in which I often missed people or things and found life in the city often challenging because it was so different. But then I also remembered, and missed, the stillness that fell in the evenings outside the second-floor apartment where I lived in the medical college, and those days when the weather was warming up, when everything, all the tasks and challenges, had been done, and one could just read. I looked back on that time as surprisingly stress free and unproblematic – not full of the usual striving and struggle that one often had in London, for instance.

But I didn't know if I would have a chance to go back soon.

———

Visits to the city over the years were often unplanned and impromptu. When I was a diplomat in Beijing, my tours back were just relatively short opportunities to notice that there were new buildings, swisher designs, and a lot more neon light at night. A gap of a couple of years meant I arrived back in the mid-2000s and noticed a really dramatic change. The centre around People's Square had been redesigned and redeveloped. The Zhaojun Hotel had been overtaken in status by a five-star Shangri-La, opposite the gates of the People's Park. In the mid-1990s, the arrival of McDonald's had been a perpetual myth that never seemed to come true. But by 2006 the whole city seemed to have its own selection of foreign fast-food brands. Above all of this towered a set of gleaming new skyscrapers. Even the roads had been rearranged and redesigned, so that the composition of the city centre was almost unrecognisable. The airport had been renovated; a highway had been completed between Beijing and the city, meaning the journey that once took almost a day to complete, driving through Shijiazhuang, was now possible in five hours. A few times as a diplomat, I undertook it, speeding along in a Land Cruiser, often experiencing newly laid roads that were largely empty of traffic. At these times, the whole of the region seemed to belong to me.

Hohhot's remodelling meant that the old place I had known came to exist only in my memory. One weekend, I decided to stay in the Zhaojun Hotel, a place that I regarded as the acme of luxury when I was a teacher, but which was now a modest three-star hotel. I spent the two days simply wandering around the city, going into the new coffee shops that had opened up, trying to retrace old paths I had taken. Strangely, I had brought a history of the punk rock movement in the UK in the 1970s to read – a book called *England's Dreaming* about the period of my life just before adolescence when this anarchic, chaotic movement with its wild energy and lack of respect for authority and rules was assaulting

British listeners.[4] I remember my grandparents being horrified when they saw performances of this kind of music. They thought civilisation had ended and a new era of barbarity had been ushered in. But of course, it proved a fad that was replaced by a different kind of music, mostly linked to electronics and computers, a few years later. And that in turn was superseded by yet more kinds of music.

The historic figure that featured most in my imagination of the city was the founder of the Yuan Dynasty, Genghis Khan – Temujin in the original rendition of his name. The iconography of the Great Khan was everywhere in the city, even though his real history was on the steppes and the vast plains and grasslands around Hohhot. Four places vied for the location of his burial tomb, and one, over the border in the Mongolian Republic, for his birth. Creator of the world's most extensive land empire, his warriors reaching the Danube in Europe, he had left an imprint on history that pervaded the popular imagination to this day. 'Horde', after all, is reportedly the only word of Mongolian origin in the English language. The representation of archers riding barebacked on horses descending on settlements throughout central Asia and into the Middle East and beyond, as though coming from thin air, was a haunting one. But so too was the extremity of violence and devastation that Khan and his successors had offered those who resisted them. In European memory, Genghis Khan was a figure of magnificence and fear, almost barely human, existing more like some mythical figure. So to be in a place where he was clearly regarded as a human, with a very clearly told human life story, was striking. In Hohhot, he was a symbol of the area, a cultural icon as much as anything else – a claim by the city and the region to global fame because of the way that Khan had simply rewritten the order of the world, and caused a redrawing of the whole map of the known planet then.

The immensity of his impact on history, at the time and thereafter, was clear to see. But because of the length of time since his life, finding authentic links to him was not easy – and certainly not available in Hohhot, which had been founded centuries after his death. The closest I could get to any sense of the world he had existed in and the milieu in which he had lived was in some of the reproductions of the kind of majestic mobile yurt which had, according to historians and archaeologists, served as his home. One of these operated as a restaurant and tourist spot just north of the city, a place where people could go for the weekend, at least in the summer, eating boiled lamb, hearing performances of Khoomei singing, and sleeping in small yurts on the grasslands. But for me, the one time I really did feel I encountered him, and the kind of aura that surrounded his personality, was when I travelled through Xinjiang in 1995. It had been an epic journey – three days by train continuously night and day from Beijing to Urumqi, then almost immediately a trip of the same length from Urumqi by sleeper bus to Kashgar, on the China-Pakistan border. Back in the autonomous region capital, I went down to Turfan, the beautiful oasis, and the Tianchi (Heavenly) Lake close by, before travelling for another day by train to a Mongolian district in Bayingolin just northeast of the region. It was when coming back from there on an eight-hour train ride that someone suggested going to the fiery mountains which had figured in the epic Ming fantasy novel *Journey to the West* mentioned above. Close to there was a small tourist spot we stopped at – a deserted city, with high earth walls, remnants of an attack that had visited annihilation on the settlement so complete that seven centuries later it was still deserted. Literature based on themes of desertion were common in English literary tradition. The Anglo Saxon work 'The Ruin' gives a haunting account of a place falling into decay after the Roman withdrawal in the fifth century, and then the slow arrival of settlers from mainland Europe. The most important city of my home area, Canterbury, had, archaeologists had found, a layer of dark earth marking the period from 400CE to around 550CE when the city had simply been neglected, only a few people living amongst its ruins, the great buildings like the Baths and the Coliseum simply crumbling.[5] The evacuation of this place had been much more complete – and meant that the remains of it were extensive and largely untouched in the intervening centuries. It was a haunting memorial to the ways in which the Mongolian conquests had impacted on the world around them, introducing new innovations in the art of war, from the use of rotten meat projected into besieged cities to spread disease to confined, resisting populations, to new developments in ballistics. That meant the historic weight of Genghis Khan was real, even in the modern city of Hohhot. And it was never difficult to find impressive renditions of his face, staring down from portraits, placed on restaurant or hotel or business walls, or on carpets knitted from locally sourced wool.

———

However, my most abiding memory of the city remained not the physical layout, or the historical links, but particular people. Of these, there were a handful who had made a deep impression. Amongst the most important was a calligraphy teacher – an elderly man who would come to my apartment once a week on a Wednesday morning, and teach me how to write Chinese characters with a pen and ink. Mr Wang had been a librarian at the college for many years, and was now retired. He had taught foreigners before but had no English, so he enjoyed chatting a bit with someone who could speak at least some Mandarin back to him. In a place of such frenetic activity, Mr Wang conveyed a remarkable tranquillity. He seemed unflustered by anything and regarded everything with complete equanimity. He had above all a remarkable writing style. My attempts to render even the simplest character, something like *ren* with its two strokes for 'man', or *da* for 'big', usually resulted in something even I could tell looked like it had been produced by a small child making their first attempts to write. When British schoolkids learn to write and then try to do joined-up writing, they take paper divided into small squares and fill each one with a separate symbol, so I did the same with a few of the main characters. Despite the most intense attention, however, the result from my pen always seemed to be unbalanced, crowded and aesthetically mediocre, even crude.

Mr Wang talked a lot about the importance of balance and posture. For him, he said, it was like wearing a hat – tilt it too far one side and it looks lopsided; tilt it too far the other side and it appears like it is about to fall off your head. He sought in everything he wrote to produce calligraphy that looked fluent and yet, in each line, expressed proportion and balance. The secret of this, he told me, was correct physical posture. He would sit almost on the edge of the chair before the desk, hold the pen in a particular way between his fingers and his thumb, dab it gently in black ink, make sure there was not too much so the result would be blotchy on the paper, and then gently, with his other arm used as a rest, let the brush flow across the page, sometimes pressing a little gently so the line thickened and the blackness darkened. In this way, Mr Wang taught me that writing in English and Chinese were, on top of all their other differences, physically very different. And while never being intrusive, he had a gentle interest in how things were in the place where I had come. His life, in many ways, had been spent amongst books, and to know him was a powerful encounter with the deep reserves and resources of Chinese culture in the life of a single person.

Searching for his home years later, I failed to find it. The city had changed so much – the streets were utterly different. Instead, I had to take refuge in a small coffee shop by the road, simply realising that some things did just fade away. One could only be grateful to know the things and experience the people one did as life went on. My final visit to the city was with a group of foreign officials, when I was serving as their tutor. We had a trip out to the Mengniu milk factory, an outfit that would have looked ultra-futuristic in my first era in the city. What was most dramatic however was the museum, which had moved from a white, two-storey building in the city out to a grand modern edifice on the way to the airport.

While I had always appreciated Hohhot as a city that had at least some history going back to the Qing Dynasty, the two museums were reminders of this far longer history – of a history under the ground, as it were, and measured in thousands of years rather than centuries. This was a history largely absent of humans and their habits. It was one that was made up of almost complete sets of skeletons found perfectly preserved in sand deserts spread across the region. It was also one that reached deep back into types of stone formation. A colleague at the medical college had made me, accidentally, aware of this when he'd asked me, and I had too readily agreed, to translate a paper he had written on the geology of the region for an international conference. The specialist vocabulary meant I waded through the piece looking up almost every other word. Even when I found them, they didn't make much sense. The one impression I got, though, was that this was a place with a wealth of geology, and that this fact was something that was internationally recognised.

The old museum had been central but small. There had only been one mammoth skeleton fully assembled in the main exhibition hall. In the new one I went to, there seemed to be an endless series of these skeletal beasts, going up along a series of halls, culminating in the largest of them, a brontosaurus, with its huge tail, long neck and cavernously large stomach enclosed in ribs, a space big enough perhaps to fit comfortably some of the tea shops I had gone to in the 1990s. Being here made me think about time. There were, everywhere, two kinds of time, I guess. Time as it figured in the immense processes and slow transformations the non-human history of the mammoths illustrated, with an immensity so great that it was almost timeless. And time as it was in the personal lives of people, with their immediate stories and the way they were creating narratives, a time that was tighter and shorter. It was hard to shift from thinking about one to considering the other – to try to connect with the deeper movements and patterns that guide one's daily affairs while being constantly distracted by the business of just being busy with the more transient, immediate things. But these two times are not separate. They do co-exist. They live alongside each other, one enclosing the other.

In many ways, Hohhot had come to belong to a particular story of a realised part of my past – a place I was now connected to by memory, rather than any ongoing, current needs. But its importance in my life and how it has developed was very clear. It was a place I went back to feeling both owned, and owning – the place where I learned most, and earliest, about the business of living in China.

BEIJING

Beijing might be vaster than Hohhot, and more important and famous, but it does have one striking thing in common – the weather. In winter months, the capital of the People's Republic can be brutally dry and cold. In summer, however, it reaches extremes that Hohhot avoids – rising one time I was there into the forties, so hot that being outside was like sitting in a sticky oven. Like Hohhot, rain is rare, but when it falls it is torrential. In the winter, too, it can snow – and snow hard.

Despite this, there are two moments of each year when the climate is perfect, and these were the occasions I most enjoyed and when I could start to appreciate the magical qualities of the city. In April just coming into the spring, the weather was neither too hot nor too cold. The air cooled in the evenings, but the days were around twenty to twenty-five degrees at most. In spring, there were green shoots on trees, and in the parks that dotted the city I could sit under the shade of trees and reimagine some of the history and the lives that had been lived in this place. In the autumn, usually late in October, a similar pleasing equilibrium returns. Nights are cool, the air conditioning during the day can go off, and there is still no need to wear coats during the evenings. Going up to a place like the Summer Palace, late in the afternoon, wandering beside the lakes there, one can feel the light breeze coming across the surface from the fragrant mountains, just visible in the distance – when the air is clear. The tourists usually disappear around four or five o'clock, and there are times like this, as dusk comes on, when the delicately painted wooden walkways come to seem like they belong only to the person sitting there. This is a nice time for dreaming, for reconnecting meditatively with the deeper currents of one's inner life. The city of over fifteen million people that is stretched around one seems quite remote. At a time and moment like this, Beijing often seems like a calm, quiet refuge.

For me, Beijing has been the place that I have most often arrived and departed from. My first ever visit to China in 1991 was to come here, landing at the second terminal of the airport, which at that time was regarded as very new, and taking a taxi in the evening to a place that seemed completely shrouded in darkness because there were so few street lights. As a new and unfamiliar place, whatever I saw on that first encounter seemed unutterably mysterious. Future visits, of course, took that impression away. By the time I transited the city in 1994 to go to live in Hohhot, it was already in the midst of another building campaign, and there were more lights, more skyscrapers, more traffic than there had been in 1991. Those few days in the city being orientated by the organisation I was working for before setting off by train to Hohhot were mostly spent rushing around, when I got the chance, with friends on the same programme, journeying in the small 'bread cars' which were ubiquitous then – ten kilometres for ten yuan was the standard tariff. But these were soon banned because of their being highly polluting. Beijing in August, the time of the year I was there then, was hot. The subway was still rudimentary, and often its stations were not convenient for the places I wanted to go. Getting from location to location was often tiring, especially because at that time I was on a minimal budget and had to take the cheapest means. When I came back in 2000, arriving in early January, things had changed, for me and for the city. This time, it was to be my home for the next three and a half years. And it meant that I had to commit to knowing its layout better, and creating a structure for my life there.

In fact, from 2000 to 2003, I worked as a British government official, a diplomat, based at what had once been the old legation in Guanghua Lu (Road), next to Ritan Park, but which was now the embassy. The embassy itself, in one of the oldest districts devoted to hosting representational entities like these, was a modest building, usually painted pink. Its main asset was an outside swimming pool, and an indoor, British-style pub called 'The Ben' (after the Westminster clock). But as the city around commercialised and developed, both of these 'luxuries' largely lost their allure because they were available on a larger scale and in more modern form elsewhere.

Embassies are often microcosms of the country where most of the people working there come from. So to work in a place like this was to exist on two planes – one very reminiscent of home, and one of the physical place where one was located. It meant that many of the people one worked with had to adopt two identities – one for their work lives, and one for when they were outside the physical confines of the embassy buildings, and getting along in the city everyone was living in. There was an anecdote about one colleague who had worked in Guanghua Lu before I had come there – a lady who had simply refused to engage much with Beijing, and had not even succeeded in getting to such iconic sites as the Great Wall or the Forbidden City during her time there. But when people spoke about this person, even though they did so in an amused and amusing way, it was clear that her attitude was regarded somewhat critically. It was a strange thing to be in one of the great urban centres of the world, and to make such an effort to block off any influence or engagement with it. That must have taken a huge amount of energy.

For me, there were two other kinds of place that I lived in for those years, beyond that of the one inside and outside the embassy I worked at. There was the Beijing that was public, grand, and political – a city of vast, sweeping boulevards that put the grand roadways imposed on Paris under Baron Haussmann in the mid-nineteenth century to shame in terms of their size, and which structured the space of the city. Alongside these were the large public buildings – government offices, hotels, shopping centres like the vast Oriental Plaza which had just been opened at the turn of the millennium in Wangfujing. This was a retail, office and hotel area, and it was often laborious to walk around – what looked like a short distance on the map could often be an epic trail. The characteristic of these kinds of spaces was that people were either transiting them, or busy going about their work, and there was little sense that they were used to lingering. In these sorts of spaces it was also rare, to the point of almost non-existence, to bump into people that one knew. In contrast to this was a city of smaller streets, hutongs, parks and places where there were opportunities to simply sit, rest, and not need to move on too quickly. Here you could see the same people doing similar things each day – children with their families playing, old people practising their exercises in the morning or at night, and people undertaking street-side trade. It was a more settled, static world, ranged around, and between, the larger, more frenetic one that almost lay over and above it.

Beijing's size meant it was often hard for me to work out the different parts of the city, and start to create an emotion towards them. Some parts, which I visited often, were initially encrusted with expectations, pre-formed opinions, and sometimes prejudices that had been acquired before even setting foot in the place. The Forbidden City typified this category – a vast series of monuments in the centre of the city, overlooking Tiananmen Square, constituting almost a city within a city. Of course, this was a terrain heavy with historic memory, the seat of imperial rulers from the Ming Dynasty onwards, and a vast monument to the symbols of their world and the way these expressed power. And once more, even starting to read these symbols adequately was a huge effort for me. Most of the time, wandering through the vast courtyards, I felt as a non-Chinese like I was part of a set for a play or a story that I didn't know the language of and had no clear idea of the key plotlines to. It was just the sheer drama of what I was moving through physically that made an impression.

As one travelled deeper into the complex, however, one came to spaces that were suggestive of a more intimate kind of lifestyle – rooms that were at least organised in ways that must have been for domestic life, with less formal décor and emphasis on protocol and reception of visitors, advisers, or officials. Gardens, exquisitely ornate, allowed you to catch your breath as you walked around. It was in these spaces that the usually large numbers of visitors, most of them from elsewhere in China, dwindled. The mighty Forbidden City, as different visits revealed manifold concealed spaces or more previously unknown areas, truly became to me a microcosm of the world around it, an embodiment in architecture of a view of the world, a vision of the way in which the universe was organised, so very different from ones from my own background.

The Great Wall was more dispersed. The three main locations were between an hour and two hours from the centre of the city by road. When I had my own car, it was easy to ride out to them, taking the newly constructed motorway that dramatically snaked its way up mountains to the north and northwest of the city, climbing up and up to ever higher ground. Badaling was the most popular and accessible, but for residents in the city it was the least alluring, simply because of the large numbers of visitors it usually received.

Mutianyu, while more distant, was preferable. Depending on the time of day I managed to get there, either on my own or with guests or friends, it was a place that could have a quiet magic – the pathway along the top of the wall between turrets quickly thinning of fellow observers so that I often found myself alone, having climbed up the steep stone steps and managed to find a place to sit and look at the woods or rocky arid places that ran beside it here.

An excursion to Mutianyu was special because it involved not just the wall, but the journey there, often past restaurants selling fish, some of which advertised facilities where you could catch your own and have them cooked. Part of the road went by dramatic gullies, with a low wall along the edges to prevent cars or buses going over the side. At others, there was a small river and a lake. The arrival at the wall itself was always a time to witness the sense of expectation of whoever I was with, especially if they had never been on this journey before. But it still took time, either to climb from the place where the ticket office was to the first stage of the wall, or catch the cable car and witness the falling away of the ground below as it swept up to the first battlements. For any non-Chinese visitor, too, making sense of the wall meant understanding a lot of new things – the kind of entity that was contained by this, and other walls, built along the northern parts of what is modern-day China, and those domains that it faced then. The assumption that the structure was of one style and period, and built against one common enemy, or for one common purpose, was the most important to remove. There were other walls – part of a family of structures, but radically different in their composition. In Inner Mongolia, I had come across one – a deeply eroded, evidently very ancient dung and mud ridge, which rose gently from the earth, and then, from time to time, disintegrated into it. The wall near Beijing had an iconic status – brick-built, evidently well cared for, a snaking, vast declaration of its status. The history here went back into the more recent Ming Dynasty, a few centuries before. Further east, the wall reached the great Bohai Sea, near Qingdao. There, it was even more dramatic – a structure reaching its termination, falling into the sea. Over in the further west, it had a history reaching back perhaps to the Qi Dynasty and the era of the First Emperor. These walls straddled such immense periods of time that the Inner Asian regions they faced, and the worlds in which they delineated an inside and an outside, were wholly different now. Their political geography had been redrawn. And the reasons for the construction of these walls also seemed various – as a means of delineating territory, as an expression of imperial status, or as a means of defensive protection. There was no one simple story they told.

The wall, with its red-bricked colours, was visually spectacular – famously so. But it was the dry brown earth that lay under the trees next to it that often impressed me, a counterpart to the colour of the main structure, something I could see when I came down from the main platform at Mutianyu, descending steps to the entrance at the base. Here, sometimes, I could hear birds call and even see them, flying from tree to tree, or through the sky – and if I had time I could wander further in amongst the trees, seeing signs of other animals, imagining more quietly the history and meaning of the place that I was in. The wall at other locations around Beijing had a different character – sometimes less restored, with fewer people, presenting more difficulty in walking along its main pathway. Still, some visitors jogged along it, others went and camped close to it, and a few brave characters walked it from east to west for as far as there was a path on it to go along. The wall, for all of its remoteness in many parts, was never a lonely or abandoned place.

Amongst my nicest memories of Mutianyu was to be there, alone with one other friend, one evening when we arrived just in time to get the final ticket for entry. It was in October, during one of the magical times of the year for Beijing, when the weather was perfect, and the city and those places near to it seemed placid and calm. The road out had been largely empty of traffic – hardly anyone had been about. The car park at the entrance to the wall was bare – mostly people getting into their cars and coaches to head away, rather than come. On the cable car up we were completely alone – as on the wall itself too. It was getting darker, and the landscape around was starting to fade into an undifferentiated stretch of darkness under massive shadows. What was most impressive, however, was the silence – almost complete, with neither the sound of traffic, nor of people, which seemed ubiquitous everywhere else. Nor animals, for that matter. The wall stretched either side, the sight of its pathway quickly evaporating into the evening and the oncoming night. We managed only a twenty-minute stay, before clambering back down in time for the very final cable car of the day. This was a reminder that the wall, for all its familiarity during the hours of light, could become a place of evocation and mystery as night came on and visibility dwindled.

———

In the city centre, there were plenty of focal points to try to build a sense of its size and geography, and over the months after 2000 I tried to get to most of them, or revisit ones I had been to before. A lot of this was done with family or friends, as a communal activity. In this context, the sights of Beijing, of the national capital, became a means of explaining, or inducting people into, the country they had often just arrived in. Places like the Temple of Heaven had a strangeness that meant they were never easy to make sense of in the first place, and then to explain to others. Of course, the parks and gardens around the key buildings were easy enough to understand, but the large circular structure in the middle, and its association with complex imperial rites, along with all the other linked buildings, usually meant the first reception was one of bafflement. How had the rites taken place? Who had been there? What had they achieved? One thing was certain even in the first moments of getting familiar with the place – it fitted no easy categories. It was not a Buddhist temple, like the ones I had seen in Hohhot, nor did it have the kinds of structures one saw in cathedrals or churches in Europe. It testified to a belief system that was obviously unique, and one that occurred in a refined, complex and very different social order.

My time in Hohhot had been largely unstructured. Teaching took up only a few hours each week. The rest of the time had been my own. In Beijing, standard office hours prevailed. Most embassy people lived in designated compounds. The oldest were in Qijiayuan or Jianguomen, by the Ming Dynasty observatory and the Second Ring Road, along which the old walls of the city had once run before being demolished in the 1950s. The apartments here were large, in blocks of flats, places for receptions and for undertaking representational work. Some colleagues lived there. I was in a newer place, the China World Hotel, opposite a group of hotels, and one of the first areas to be developed in the early 1990s. I knew this place from my time in Hohhot, coming here sometimes on the overnight train, arriving early in the morning at the nearby Beijing Railway Station, vast and forever busy, walking up to one of the Western eateries nearby to remind myself of the taste of fast food at home. In the final days in Beijing before coming back to the UK in 1996, a friend of a friend from America had kindly loaned their flat, and its décor, the size of the television, the air conditioning, everything seemed to epitomise modernity and luxury – even the existence of English-language cable television.

Transiting Beijing a couple of times before moving back to

live there in 2000, I had been a business person, sourcing food products from factories in the country. On one visit I had taken an epic route from Hong Kong to Fuzhou to look at asparagus production, then from Fuzhou by train to Nanning in Guangxi province to look at pineapples, which were grown, canned, and exported from there. After Nanning, with its fields of fruits, bamboo groves, and semi-tropical climate, I flew to Hangzhou on the eastern side, to inspect water chestnuts in a modernised factory that produced some of the finest vegetarian food I'd ever tasted. From there I went by car to Hefei, capital of the central Anhui province, and from Hefei up by train overnight to Taiyuan. Here, in the heart of the northern province of Shanxi, one of the great historic centres of the country, I was driven out to walnut production farms, and told about the oily, tasty attributes that made the produce from here some of the most sought after in the world. They also grew garlic, and exported it in powder form, or in small dry slices. A brief trip to Hohhot, and I was back in Beijing, recovering from so much travel for a couple of days by indulging myself in one of the steakhouses of China World Hotel. This was the place that was to end up, a mere two years later, and in an entirely different occupation, as my home for three and a half years.

China World Hotel was only a few minutes' walk to the embassy. In the mornings, I would come down in the lift to the grand marble entrance and walk up to Guanghua Lu, the street running east to west, where, after walking along past a couple of intersections, the embassy came into sight. Even in a small section of the outside world like this, the smells I experienced varied. Those that came from a small eatery serving breakfast snacks, or from an outlet selling the fried pieces of dough from a large wok of boiling oil that many liked to eat on their way to work, were strong and obvious. Others were more subtle and momentary: the faintest hint of incense passing by the opened window of someone's house on the ground floor. Or the whiff of someone's perfume as they marched by, on their way to some office work or first appointment of the day. Fruit stalls, even in the winter months, carried their own aromas and scents. The edge of the road was full of bicycles, meaning I had to divert, walk around them, sometimes step into the road. The cars during the morning walk were endless, sometimes sounding their horns, particularly around the main junction. But miraculously, most of the time things kept moving. Depending on the time of year, the air had a specific quality and feel, which was more than just about its smell. In winter, it could be very dry, so that often when you touched metal you got a small, alarming shock from static. In summer, things became humid, the light could be stark, glaring, and it was a case of finding the shady side of the street, or wandering a little indirectly along backstreets that were more shadowy, and which provided surprisingly tranquil ways of making it to the area around the embassies. In the hottest weather, when the preoccupation was simply to get from one air-conditioned oasis to another, passing even the smallest shop meant I could feel a little of their cool air inside escaping into the world around them, lapping at my skin like it was cool water from a pool.

The inside of the embassy, the usual destination each morning, had a particular décor – white walls, a royal crest on the wall facing me as I came in, cool air in the summer, and warm in winter. It was usually peaceful, almost as though there were no other people working there. My room was at the end of one of the ground corridors, so unless someone made the deliberate choice to come and find me, there was no reason for people to be passing by. There I could sit at my desk and look out over the small courtyard in front, with trees, a wall, and some bicycles parked in a shed. Some days there were events to go to outside – meetings with officials, accompanying visitors, or simply making reports. People visited, some from within China, some from the UK or elsewhere abroad. Often there were fellow diplomats to speak to, or journalists, or Chinese or foreign colleagues and friends. As often as I could, I went on visits to other parts of the country. There was, after all, more to China than Beijing.

———

Beijing was a place of the obviously man-made: buildings, roads, underpasses, shopping centres, and restaurants, that was true. But it also had attempts to preserve or emulate (even if heavily managed) nature. Parks were the main spaces for this. It was here that I had the space to try to contemplate things and see something of the lives of people who lived in the city and called it their native home, because at least here there were no vehicles, and people had to walk and appear in the daylight. Parks in cities like London were often displays of an idea of the natural world in amongst places that were so evidently human creations. But this stark dichotomy – humans and the natural world – was based on ideas that were massive simplifications, constructions as it were, creating polarity where there should have been a spectrum in between. The great parks of London or Paris were products of particular human ideas about how the world of nature should look – a civilised, ordered, and often controllable world. They

were driven by an aesthetic underpinned by a host of philosophical and social ideas, of what was beautiful, what looked
good, what was pleasing to the idea. The British landscape,
for all its famous beauty and 'naturalness', had been planned,
manipulated and created by humans for centuries, so that
even the most wild-looking wood, or epically presented park
or grassland was populated by trees, shrubs and plants that
had been specially planted, and features that were the result
of intervention, not organic growth.[1]

The parks of Beijing, as I discovered each of them, offered
lessons in the order, society, and culture of the place, in ways
that were far more educational than going, for instance, to a
museum or an exposition. Here, depending on the time of
day I went, there were young children with their grandparents looking after them, or elderly people simply doing their
exercises, or, in the late afternoon, practising taijiquan, and
even dancing in some areas. In Ritan Park, right next to the
embassy, there was a space where an elderly man held a long
brush as he stood and wrote characters in water on the pave-
ment – phrases, poems, sentences that disappeared slowly as
the liquid they were written in evaporated, a beautiful image
of human transience. The park was a place of movement and
sights, but also of sounds – of people sometimes singing,
often Beijing Opera, or of someone performing on the *erhu*, a
two-stringed instrument that typifies the sound of traditional
music. The division of space in Ritan Park was like that of
most of the others in the city – small enclosed areas that lead
from one to the other after the entrance through the main
gate interspersed by larger more monumental areas. In one
place were rock structures, shapes punctuated by holes,
contorted, sculpted and manipulated. In another, one entered
a shadowy bamboo grove, often so densely populated with

plants that it seemed like night-time under the leaves, even in the heart of the day. There were areas of wood, trees equally spaced apart, and places where pools of water contained swimming, colourful fish, visible just under the surface of the water. On the edges, and in the very centre of Ritan there were tea shops, and a restaurant where from time to time I met friends for lunch.

Every park I went to had specific features, things that made each one different and memorable, or memories of things that happened in them that stayed with me. Beside the almost permanently busy complex of the Forbidden City there were small gates facing Tiananmen Square. In the western one lay Zhongshan Park, named after Sun Yatsen, the first president of the Republic of China when the Qing Dynasty fell in 1911-1912. For somewhere so central, it was intriguing why this place was always so calm and had few people in it. Even better were the old buildings close to its centre, though to find these one had to follow a maze-like group of paths through similar wood and water and sculpture features present in other parks. The main function of these places was to act as concert halls, though I never saw any performances there, nor, for that matter, any sign of people coming and going to attend musical events. In the winter, this place had a particular attraction – a back area where you could look over the frozen waters around the solemn, grand brick walls at the perimeter of the Forbidden City. I some- times imagined as I came here what it would be like to conceal yourself and wait till the doors were locked and you had the place to yourself. Even so, there were times during the day when it seemed like I was the only person there – in a city of over fifteen million, right at its heart, and completely alone.

There were plenty of other parks across Beijing – some small, tucked away, others large, built around important buildings. The new opera house – the National Centre for the Performing Arts – in construction when I was there, with its vast glass dome and the dozens of different halls and concert venues stretching out over what must have been acres, had a series of fountains and landscaped spaces stretching in each space west, south, north or east from it. And of course, for longer walks, one could spend afternoons into evenings in the grounds of the Summer Palace, with the waters lapping against the marble walkways, and the flutter of birds rising and falling onto the surface of the water.

Public spaces where movement was arrested were often a refuge in a place where everything seemed to be enervated by an endless energy and motion. Cars dominated the city now more than ever. When I rode a bike, I found it far more intimidating than in Hohhot. The highways were wider, the distances longer, and the traffic fiercer, even if less speedy. Walking too was often not easy. Distances between underground stations at that time, before the Beijing Olympics saw so many new lines opened, were often huge. And I was unfamiliar with the bus routes, and never really dared to use them. When I did walk, therefore, the shopping malls and spaces where anyone could enter, like the lobbies of hotels and large museums, offered a kind of sanctuary, a place to find somewhere to sit and observe things around me. The ice skating rink in the basement of China World Hotel opposite my apartment was one favourite place, largely because there were a lot of other people there with the same intention and idea, and because of the sheer entertainment of seeing skaters who ranged from complete beginners to what looked, at least to me, to be almost professional level. The ways in which such completely different kinds of expertise levels managed to mix in one space said a lot about the diversity of China – enormous variations even in one field and one space. One small boy almost crawled across the ice once, sprawling, veering, precariously tipping forward, while more fluent movers steered their way expertly around him, and one, a girl who looked a little older than him, went pirouetting by, like she was taking part in a world championship final. The really striking thing was the patience of people, the lack of any irritation or anger, at least from the way they responded or behaved, to people of far inferior ability sometimes getting in their way by falling over or moving so slowly in front of them. What impressed me most of all was the total insouciance on the expressions of the most skilled skaters faces by the effects of incompetent ones around them and the accidents that befell them. They carried on as though nothing were happening, a look of serene concentration on their faces. I knew the one I would be if I was there on the surface of the ice – the incompetent, unable to find balance, grasping the bars at the edge of the rink in terror, watching enviously while the more talented went zipping by with effortless ease.

One of the focal refuge points was Beijing Hotel, a place familiar to me under a number of guises. It was the place I kept returning to when I had my first visit to Beijing in 1991, its restaurants at least dependable because they had English menus at a time when I was helplessly unable to speak or read any Chinese at all. These days, though, Beijing Hotel was this amalgam of different buildings, with the Grand Hotel to the most westerly part, a place where we often as diplomats accommodated our VIP guests. The more useful thing about this part of the building though was the bar at the top, cool in the evening, even after the hottest of days, and with this exhilarating view over the Forbidden City laid out before it, trees crowded around its main buildings, and only a few lights suggesting the magnitude and magnificence of the buildings, submerged in night darkness. Sitting here, I got some idea of the proper geography of the city, the ways in which the centre, through restrictions, had no high-rise buildings out of respect for the ancient properties, but how quickly things developed, so that further west in what was now the financial district there were bright office blocks and glaring nights lighting up the horizon.

Beijing Hotel proper, next door, had been one of the earliest places where foreigners had been able to stay during the few visits by Westerners into the country from 1949 to the end of the 1970s. Some people I knew back in the UK had been part of the delegations that came here, and resided in the rooms the hotel offered. One of them had been a journalist based here in the early 1980s. It was one of the few places permitted to accommodate non-Chinese. That gave the hotel the air almost of a concession or a compound. It was only years later, however, that I myself actually managed to stay there, in around 2009, when just on a whim I booked online one of the standard rooms, to see what it was like. The décor was nothing out of the ordinary for a hotel in the centre of a major Chinese city catering to business people and tourists. However, the height of the ceilings and the atmosphere of the place were different from anywhere else I had ever stayed – and even the most careful attention to the thick curtains could not exclude some of the bright light coming in from the streets, even in the middle of the night, or the sounds of a city forever, these days, on the move. I felt that I was in the muffled centre of a vastly busy crossing point. The other hotel that came to have meanings accrued to it was The Friendship Hotel, once way out on the Third Ring Road, almost in the place where the city ended and the surrounding countryside began, but increasingly now nestled in amongst university, business and shopping districts as Beijing has grown in size. The hotel had been built in the 1950s when the Soviet Union sent experts to China. After political ruptures between the two countries, it became home to people of other nationalities who were still coming to the city. In the mid-1990s, it had served as the offices and country headquarters of the organisation I worked for, and therefore a place I tended to gravitate to when I came to the capital. I liked the place – the architecture of the shallow apartments around the main hotel building was restrained, refined, almost like the quads at an Oxbridge college. There were small gardens and playing areas in between these, and an enormous Olympic-sized swimming pool. At the back, the classical Chinese architecture, or a modern copy of it, dominated, in a huge reception hall and restaurant. This was a place I had to make an effort to come to, because even in the early 2000s it had no easy public transport links. But with a car, it was easy enough to find, a journey almost direct from China World Hotel on the Third Ring Road round from east to west, to the compound the hotel was in. It was also easy to park there, before any real restrictions were imposed.

Most times I went to the hotel, I either sat in the lobby coffee area, reading books, or went into the bar at the side, a TGI Fridays from quite early on, where I could meet friends. It was an easy place for people to find and a convenient rendezvous if they were also driving. I could imagine the way this place must have been like a world on its own in the past. It had shops (some of the few in 1995 that sold relatively decent Western-style bread), and a park, and places to simply sit and be ignored. There was even a bamboo grove, rustling in the wind, and a Korean restaurant, over near the front gate. Again, it was only much later, as an academic in Australia, that I stayed as a guest in the hotel part of the complex – and once again, the rooms were standard. What else was I expecting? The place had a sentimental meaning, though, after all the times I had visited. But as a diplomat, it was also somewhere in the city, but a little apart from it, where I could go and feel I was displaced from the sometimes claustrophobic and quite intense atmosphere of the embassy.

———

Finding refuges anywhere matters. In Beijing, because of the association with politics and power, a lot of time was spent in government buildings, visiting, seeing officials, taking minsters on visits, or simply transacting official business. The Great Hall of the People was a common venue – a place where I managed to see figures like Zhu Rongji, the premier in the late 1990s, or visiting dignitaries like British politicians. I even went there once to sit in the main auditorium and see a performance of George Gershwin's opera *Porgy and Bess* – a strange clash between American modern music and the highly formal setting of what was normally a large meeting room for congress members. Once I entered up the steps from Tiananmen Square, I saw the Hall had immense walkways with carpets, and this hushed atmosphere as though, no matter how many people were there, I felt I was in a place where everyone had taken a vow of silence. Perhaps even if I shouted out loud there, no one would hear me, so effective were the softening effects on any sound of the wall, ceiling and floor coverings.

Other buildings where governance went on were more functional. The old Ministry of Foreign Affairs, where a foreign relations think tank had been based from the 1990s, had a pleasant set of courtyards and what must have been late Qing Dynasty buildings around them, full of wood carvings and ornaments. This was a good place for hushed, intricate discreet discussions. The new ministerial building was a larger, more visible affair, though it too, on its ground floor, had meeting rooms where similar kinds of discussion could happen. I realised that parts of Beijing's less visible face, much like London's, were found through these entrances and doors that led into rooms where you could talk and act more intimately. The public buildings and spaces, like the vast Tiananmen Square right at the heart of the city, were sometimes a façade, a distraction. The places I tried to go most of the time I was a diplomat, and for all the periods afterwards, were those in which people in the city became more knowable, and talk more meaningful and direct.

Of all these experiences in the official side of Beijing, the visits to Zhongnanhai were the most anticipated and the most prestigious. The government compound outer walls were visible enough from the road. I had even walked by its main southern gate many times, with three soldiers standing in olive uniforms before the door, so still it was like they were made of wax, with the huge letters in the calligraphy of Mao Zedong on the front wall behind them declaring to any car or delegation that entered: 'Serve the People'. As a diplomat, visits were not common, but they did happen. And the transition from the usually dizzily busy Chang An Avenue outside, with its twelve lanes for traffic, and the immense calm almost the moment one was in the compound was always startling. The buildings here were historic, something that was obvious even for someone with little idea of how to interpret traditional Chinese architecture. They spoke of an imperial past, where this region had been the domain of emperors and their courtiers. These days, there were more modern buildings speckled about the place, but they seemed to keep a respectful distance from the main reception buildings, which were able to maintain a sort of spatial aloofness. On my visits, usually as the most junior member accompanying delegations with political or business figures, the colours of the rooms and halls, the ways in which they were decorated with so many motifs that I had seen in other Chinese art or museums, fascinated me. When my mind wandered during the discussions I had to listen in to, I would look at the patterns and the motifs around me and try and work out what this all meant, what kind of world it spoke from. Of course, it was easy to just accept what one saw as different, Chinese, exotic, belonging to a world that was unfamiliar and therefore dealt with best by simply labelling it like that. But the consistency of the symbols, the small, circuitous images of dragons on the roof eaves or the delicately drawn and painted foliage on wooden decoration within for instance, were evidently derived from a collective language of the imagination and a common aesthetic, and linked to histories of interpretable symbols, arising from a world in which these had consistent meaning.

The most striking characteristic standing in Zhongnanhai, the sensation that was most prevalent, was the stillness, especially in the hot weather. One had come from a world of almost perpetual motion and movement, but a simple journey through the main gateway somehow muffled all of this. And this stillness seemed to pervade everything, even the surface of the lake water, which was forever unruffled, at least when I stood there observing it. There were birds flying past, and sometimes the faint rustle of wind in the trees, but that was about all. Unlike the public paths and other locations of Chinese nature, here there were no clusters of people or crowds. The grass on the small lawns was correctly cut, the roads very clean, and the steps up to the meeting hall with its grand entrance always absolutely pristine. I could not see the world around me, even though I was in a massive city. The compound had a complete calmness about it. It reminded me of the description Edgar Snow gave on one of his later visits to China as an old man, when he met Mao in his rooms. As he left, he noticed no one around, saw no particular signs of security, and was able to wander across the small grassed area back to his own lodgings that night as though he and the nation's leader were the only two people staying there.[2]

Back in amongst the traffic, it was like rising up from the quiet depths of water into noisy air. North of the Forbidden City, up towards the Drum Tower, a remnant of the city walls, bars and small streets weaved their way around the canal areas. This was a particular haunt of expats in the city, a place to take visitors, because it had a great atmosphere. It seemed to be populated with ghosts from the past, very tangible ones. There was even a Lu Xun restaurant in the time I lived there, serving dishes mentioned in his works. Houhai Lake, as darkness came on, was a good place to let the mind wander, to sit there alone or with friends, and sip beers, letting the smells of these backstreets and the water waft past. There was a large, popular duck restaurant right at the edge of the main lake whose kitchens contributed disproportionately to the aromas. Being close to water brought cooling freshness when it was humid and hot. In winter, there were times when I could watch people skate here, a more picturesque setting than the basement of China World Hotel.

I did wonder when I was able to pass time here, how you could put all the separate pieces of the city together, a city as vast and full of life, and with a history as long and complex, as this one. Did you just live with the component parts running alongside each other and tolerate their divergences, or try to place them together and make a coherent whole. The poet WB Yeats had argued in his later life that until wisdom came to him with age, he had lived four different lives – as a poet, activist, lover, and traveller – but that the great mission had been to unify and harmonise these. Harmony was a powerful, evocative word in Chinese, one around which, to use the language of the philosopher Ludwig Wittgenstein, there was an immense language game, defined by the use of the word in the many different contexts it was deployed, and with roots reaching back to the first occurrence of the term in the philosophies of the Warring States thinkers, 2,400 years before. Because of this history and link with very specific systems of thought from Chinese traditions, I often felt *hexie* (harmony) was one of the most important words in the Chinese language you had to work out a specific meaning for, because it did differ so much from the language game of the same word in English. It had a different cultural, theological, social and political context. In China, this question of harmonising things and putting everything, for all their difference, together, in a sort of order really stood out not just as a great personal task, but also as an immense public one. It was linked to notions of how the world was, in itself – a belief in things being aligned between the natural and the human in a way that was truthful and real. If you worked out the language game around harmony in Chinese, you were well on your way to gaining a deeper entry and insight into almost every aspect of the Chinese world around you. You could, as it were, build a whole world up from this one term.

On my earliest visit to China, I had gone one afternoon to the Confucian Temple along some quiet backstreets in the city. I never revisited that place, but I did often go to the Lama Temple, with its splendid red-tiled, sloping decorated roofs standing conspicuously by the Second Ring Road northern part, and the gigantic wooden standing Buddha in the main hall, rising up like some mythical figure into the incense-smoke-filled roof, its eyes glaring down. Confucianism and Buddhism had been part of the three great teachings, along with Daoism, with its celebrating of contradictory forces clashing with each other and creating a world of dynamic energy. The belief systems of Chinese people had always puzzled foreigners. During his account of his mission to China from Great Britain in 1793-1794, the British envoy Lord Macartney had complained several times about being unable to understand what his hosts in Peking, as the city was called then, were intending, and working out how they thought. With other Europeans, there were common values, common Christian symbols and a shared literature and often even a common mythology. Even with the Islamic world there was the simplicity of dealing with a community that abided by theism – albeit a different kind of theism from the one that dominated in Europe. With China, though, nothing seemed the same with the imperial Chinese system that prevailed at the time of Macartney's visit. Everything was different, from the view of the world, to the language used, and the way that language organised and arranged the world.[3]

The search for unity, however, was not alien to Chinese intellectual traditions, despite the balance between the three great teachings through the last millennium and a half of Chinese histories. Kang Youwei, one of the most celebrated of the early reformers at the very final stage of the Qing Dynasty, had even produced a book of synthesis, called *The Great Unity* (*Da Tong*), an attempt to marry Western and Eastern thought systems together. In the twentieth century, the task had continued through figures like Carl Jung, the psychologist, who had dipped into Eastern thought systems and used Eastern symbols, as already mentioned, many of them tracing back to the *I Ching*, in his own account of the collective unconscious and the symbols patterning this. For me, a sole individual in this city, the principal issue was how to harmonise my experiences of places like Houhai Lake, Zhongnanhai or the Forbidden City in ways that were not alienating, which at least accommodated and assimilated them coherently with my other experiences, but also were respectful of their real variances from what I had experienced before too. How to find an authentic language that managed this balancing act?

There was one option, but one I resisted. I could have become a divided self, someone with a Chinese and then a foreign outlook, switching from one to the other like changing a hat. That would have meant a sort of bipolarity, where part of my brain ended up thinking of ways I would claim were 'Chinese' and the other in Western ways. Francois Jullien, in a superb book on the dialogue between Western and Eastern thought, based on his twenty years living in

China, described the difference between these intellectual and emotional differences as between a Western desire to always be aiming for objectives, results and conclusions, traced back to the great argumentative tradition of the Greco-Romans, and that of the Warring States period philosophers Mencius, Confucius, Mo Zi, Han Fei and others. Jullien argued that their desire was to simply see a receptive, accommodating and more passive acceptance of reality – a case of acknowledging one's limitations, being able to acknowledge the order and harmony of the world and work within it, jettisoning the idea of neat outcomes and destinations, either for thought or action. Jullien characterised this as a Western philosophical tradition that was subjective and placed the ordering and rationalisation intellect almost apart from the world, and a Chinese one that simply had the mind in the world, as part of the world, occupying a place in the great hierarchy of being.

Jullien commences *A Treatise on Efficacy* with: 'To what extent have we ever stepped outside that European schema or are we even able to – can we even question it ('we' within the European tradition who still perpetuate those early Greek categories)? ... We set up an idea form (eidos), which we take to be a goal (telos) and we then act in such a way as to make it become fact .... We chose to intervene in the world and give a form to reality.'[4]

Chinese thought, though, he argues, 'is a way out of our rut, for it never constructed a world of ideal forms, archetypes, or pure essences that are separate from reality but inform it. It regards the whole of reality as a regulated and continuous process that stems purely from the interaction of the factors in play (which are at once opposed and complementary: the famous yin and yang).'[5]

It was always easy to know a little in Beijing, and be able

to assume that I had unlocked with my 'Chinese' mind the correct interpretation of what was before me. But the longer I stayed in the city, the more I saw it as a place of layers, different kinds of geography and arrangements of space, even different feelings about what space was. In some places, like Houhai Lake, things seemed infinite once darkness came, the physical boundedness of objects simply disappearing. You could see stars in the sky, and faint lights of objects that might be near or far, and it was unclear what people were around you. But in other places, space was confined, particularly in parks where foliage, sculpture and water features interrupted paths, dictated where movement was possible, and sometimes, as in the northern part of the Forbidden City, made the world simply close in so that it seemed to consist of me, only me, the individual, confined in tightly circumscribed space.

The great modern art historian and poet Frank O'Hara had once written rapturously a line about 'grace to live life as variously as possible'. And Beijing, like London, had variety – that much was common between them. It was this quality of variousness therefore that I focused on to get through the impasse of ending up with a fractiously divided brain. And variousness meant a knowledge that was not riven and discomforted by this, but energised and strengthened. It was easy to bring a set of assumptions by which to interpret the landscape around me which just made it strange and alien. Beijing, after all, was seemingly heavy with clues in its physical layout and the order and arrangement of its buildings, of a kind of view of order and power that was different from the one I knew back in Europe. Large boulevards divided the city up in this highly assertive way, and the vast public space at the heart of it, Tiananmen Square, was a territory resplendent with different memorials of former leaders, former happenings, former presences, all from a different historical narrative. Despite these markers, the square was also just a space, emptiness that imagination was invited to fill.

One could accumulate assumptions in the West about how Chinese aesthetics were impersonal, that landscapes were frequently portrayed without human figures, that there was a sort of collectivist predisposition, a Buddhist-derived nihilism in the culture that was conveyed by its pervasive symbols. The even more fateful trap was to be seduced by notions of exoticism, of the mystical orient, the kind of mindset that Edward Said had described and attempted to counter in his deeply influential 1970s book *Orientalism*.[6] Things were different in this landscape I was in, for sure, but it was how one managed and understood those differences, and what sort of weight one gave them that mattered most. After all, from the UK, the style and idiom of French classical architecture and literature can seem even more esoteric. So close, it should be the same, or more similar. Why is it so different? China at least had the excuse of physical, historical and cultural distance to explain its differences.

In fact, years later, reading books by scholars deeply schooled in Chinese philosophy, like Donald Munro's magnif-icent set *The Concept of Man in Early China* and *The Concept of Man in Contemporary China*, made it clear that one of the most fundamental divergences were around conceptualisations – not of things or objects but of the self in the Chinese tradi-tion and that which prevailed for much of the history of the West. The concept of the self in classical Chinese texts did not give the idea that the identity of this was derived from occupying a place in a social hierarchy where validation came from external factors, and was based on assessment of status and ability as it was in the West (something Munro imputes to the influence of Plato and Aristotle). It was more embedded in a notion, in his words 'that men are naturally equal'.[7] At the heart of this was the idea that 'all men have an evaluating mind; this is the key to understanding the Confucian concept of man'. Therefore, 'the sole criterion for receipt of political and economic privilege was merit', where all humans had the capacity, through diligent copying of the right models and training, to become 'gentlemen' or 'gentle-women' – people of moral probity and standing, no matter what worlds they came from.[8] That underpinned the Confucian exam system that prevailed till the end of the Qing Dynasty – the immense meritocratic exercise which many took, some several times, in order to serve in the imperial bureaucracy.

Perhaps I was able to adopt this Chinese notion of a self, one that had the intrinsic ability, no matter what its background and history, to understand and be accepted into this Beijing environment, and to be received as an equal there. In any case, even attempting this gave another viewpoint, a different view of the world, and that diversification was enriching and valuable. Why not, after all, use an attitude modelled on something written in the Confucian era, maybe by the Master himself – the 'Great Learning', the constant ability to be open, available, and flexible to sensations and ideas. Beijing in that way taught me that there were no iron bonds around the self – and that, in many ways, the city here was as much mine as it was anyone's, even though I was not native to it. There were no restrictions on ownership, despite what initially seemed like forbidding cultural boundary walls and parameters. Those were merely things my assumptions had put there – they were never, and had never been, objective, and I could, with patience and effort, think through them.

———

One of the most intimate places in the city, if one managed to get there on days when there were few visitors, was the mansion once owned by imperial Prince Gong. This too lay amidst some hutongs which had been preserved, not far from the aforementioned Houhai Lake. When the weather was cool, this place was a delight, but it had a significance beyond being a splendid, well preserved Ming Dynasty mansion. It was associated, reportedly, with the family of the great writer Cao Xueqin. He was the author of the main portion of the greatest, and most loved, of Chinese classical novels, *The Dream of the Red Mansions*. The book, in 120 chapters, which in its superb English translation by David Hawkes and his son-in-law John Minford ran to five volumes, also goes under the name of *The Story of the Stone*.

Cao figured in my life wholly accidentally, and much earlier than my Beijing years. In a wholly nondescript bookshop in Dartford, the town in Kent where I had gone to secondary school, I had been flicking through the very few Penguin Classics books there one day, when I came across one with a beautiful Chinese portrait on the cover. This was the first volume of the translated *The Story of the Stone*. The other four I got later. But the first reading of it, or attempt to read it, was baffling. It sat neglected on my bookshelf for several years afterwards, until, studying Chinese intensively in London in 1993, I reread the first volume and then marched through the rest of the book. I remember this clearly because I did it while holidaying in a friend's house in the South of France, in the Lot et Garonne region. The place was one of great atmosphere, isolated, with a huge lawn before the old farmhouse, where I could sit on a deck chair and slowly move through the immense novel.

It was not easy, even in such an ideal setting. And while I retained enough to remember the epic, torturous and ultimately tragic romance between the protagonist Jia Baoyu (reportedly based on Cao) and Lin Daiyu, much of the detail of the novel, and the intricate description of social interaction it contained, was beyond me – especially as it was probably impossible to even remotely render into English. While living in Hohhot, I remember one of the most popular dramatisations of the novel ran on television for a few weeks over the summer. But following it was like engaging with something completely new – it didn't seem to bear any relation to the novel I had struggled through a few years before.

In Beijing, in the early 2000s, and then on a subsequent visit years later, being in Gong's mansion at least made the world of the novel a bit more tangible and comprehensible. It was clear to me that my Chinese friends who had read and admired the book had a particular common characteristic – they all enjoyed the language and dense interlinking of references, allusions, and the suggestiveness underlying the characters used, which echoed with other portions in the book, and had a specific quality that made reading it such a pleasure. The language was evidently a core part of the magic and joy of reading the work rather than merely following the plot, something a little similar to the way that Shakespeare is about more than just the bald narratives of his great plays, most of which, after all, were borrowed from other sources. Shakespeare's language, its variety, and the depth and range of the different registers given to people, was the source of his compelling hold over readers through the centuries since his death.

The parallel between Shakespeare and his prominence in Western culture and that of Cao in Chinese is not simply about influence afterwards and critical evaluation. Cao shared with the British author a kind of illusiveness. One critic speaking to me of the book one evening in Beijing said that it contained a number of different kinds of voices, and that readers tended to navigate the work by extracting very individual and particular meanings that were relevant to them and their inner lives and the challenges they faced. There was no such thing as a singular Cao voice or style, but many different, equally compelling, equally authentic-sounding ones. A similar claim is made for the immense diversity of views and attitudes and voices in Shakespeare's corpus. For lovers, *The Story of the Stone* was a manual for love. For politicians, it was an account of the shifts in human relations and the impact this has on the distribution of power between people. Those of a more metaphysical bent could find a description, particularly in the first parts of the book, of a spiritual world above the physical one humans inhabit – another order of reality, testified by the speaking stone and the mystical jade that ends up in the protagonist Jia Baoyu's mouth at the time of his birth. Cao himself seems barely known – although many claim that Jia's story is so intricately and intimately told it must be based on the author's own and that there is a heavy element of autobiography in the work. In this elusive quality, as with Shakespeare, for whom contemporary documentary evidence, while reasonably plentiful, offers no insights into the writer's personality and habits beyond his business affairs, Cao's own biography is hardly known. As with Shakespeare, too, there are complex questions over authorship, with some plays now recognised as being co-authored or revised and adapted by the playwright with some of his contemporaries. For *The Story of the Stone*, while the first eighty chapters are accepted as being penned by Cao, the final forty were probably by a slightly later author, Gao E, replicating the style of the original, but, in the view of many, not quite meeting its standards.

This ghostly quality of Cao comes across when moving around Gong's mansion. It was tempting to think of this as being the place on which he based the location of his novel – that, after all, was about the lives of a group of related families in courtyard complexes just like these in the Qing capital. But whether it really did figure as the physical space where Cao imagined his story unfolding is impossible to say – and as strange a thing to think much about as the vexed questions of whether houses in Rochester High Street in Kent, for instance, were the 'location' of events that 'happened' in Dickens' fiction. When I saw plaques celebrating that this was the place where the opening scenes of *Great Expectations* occurred, they only begged the question for me of how things that never actually happened could be commemorated in a real place.

The urge to think of Gong's mansion as the 'real location' is a strong one, however. And going around its small enclosed and delicately arranged separate gardens, culminating in the final one with a great stone feature rising up from the small pond surrounding it, I could imagine scenes from the novel becoming tangible – places in the current building where the family and their associates held their poetry reading evenings, or where poor Jia was fiercely beaten by his father for being a miscreant. Wang Xifeng, one of the most vivid, imperious figures in the novel, might appear, I thought, dressed in the clothing one imagines was worn at the time, gained from paintings and museum artefacts.

As the capital city, Beijing, like any major city similar to it, had a representational function. From the 2000s, much was being built – new structures were being erected. Going to work in the morning, on that walk along Guanghua Lu, I went by a couple of building sites, one dormant, the building at night dark and unlit against the sky, the other being clambered over by builders putting up sometimes a layer a day, with bamboo scaffolding clad across the façade. The city was daily changing; the American embassy was moving, with much fanfare, from its location near us to a designated space, much larger and more modern and grander, further out by the Third Ring Road. Modernity in Beijing was sometimes more confronting than even in the most avant-garde of European cities. In my time there, the National Centre for the Performing Arts of China, vast and surreal as it rose in a dome west of the Great Hall of the People, was completed. The third terminal of the new airport was already being planned; within a few years, just before the 2008 Olympics, it started to receive planes. The first arrival I made here was bewildering – staring up at the ceiling with its bronze-coloured parallel lines far above, and looking towards exits so far ahead that when there was smog or fog, it actually obscured the internal distances, just as it would in the outside world. The headquarters of China Central Television, designed in part by the Dutch architect Rem Koolhaas, was in the preliminary stages soon after my 2000 arrival. The real spurt of modernist city development though was to wait till after I left the city, in April 2003, to work back home. That was when Olympic construction began in earnest.

I had started as a diplomat late in my career, in my early thirties, unlike many of my colleagues who had joined just after they graduated from university in their early twenties. For me, therefore, there was a generic issue common to all people from outside of China working there – the way in which the city sometimes divided up so starkly between traditional and much more recent structures. But there was also an added component specific to me, of there always being two layers of experience from my personal narrative in Beijing I was mindful of – that of the present, being driven into and out of ministries in embassy-number-plated cars, living a life that many saw as privileged and mysterious (even though much of the time it was neither), and of the former stories and encounters in this city I had had before, as a teacher or a traveller, a business person, where the whole place seemed wholly different and was driven by different dynamics. For those who had only ever been officials there, I realised that much of what they saw would have veered between the traditional and ultra-modern Beijing and belonged to the first group above. This would have given them a somewhat polarised view of the city. At least my accounting was more complicated, and less easy to classify.

For the traditional city, as a diplomat, there were specific places that figured often, and seemed to be shared as venues to use by many others in the same vocation. Places like the preserved Sichuan Restaurant, for instance, one of the oldest larger restaurants in the city, a place where visitors could sit in the courtyard outside, or in the cool wooden building within, and gingerly peck at food smothered in ominous-looking chillies – sometimes so completely that no other ingredient was in sight.[9] Lao She's tea house, by Qianmen Gate, was another popular destination where we seemed to be forever taking visitors too, evoking ideas of the old-style city – named after the great writer of the twentieth century who had lived in London as a young man, and then tragically died in the Cultural Revolution. The Beijing Opera delivered here at least had a running English translation on an electronic board, and the luxury of waiters running at people's beck and call between the tables while performers sang and delivered snacks and tea. Further south from Qianmen Gate, at the southern end of Tiananmen, there were less formal parts of old Beijing – a huge dumpling restaurant, which became a particular favourite for more casual, less high maintenance visits, and then places I came to like which I discovered more by myself, drawn to them by their smell from the main street. One in particular sold Xinjiang-style food – the spicy kebabs, and the dishes of lamb, with nan bread, or what was called Xinjiang salad – tomatoes and lettuce, mostly. For the modern city, that was the space where the majority of the government or business meetings happened, where one went to see other diplomats. It consisted of the offices of most multinational companies or international organisations, and many of the embassies themselves – ones like the Australian, with its bold stark administrative building facades around an entry courtyard, or the even more futuristic residence of the Dutch ambassador, full of glass, and chic marrying of the garden with the building itself. Areas like Xidan or Finance Street close by were riotous with gleaming new structures like these. Again, it was the Olympics that brought this to a head, with the complex shapes of the Bird's Nest Stadium and the National Aquatics Centre taking pride of place, a counterweight against more traditional buildings, and offering something that could make a claim to be Chinese architectural modernity.

Tellingly, one of the most effortlessly patronised haunts for embassy people looking after visitors was the Liqun Roast Duck Restaurant, hidden along some hutongs (another Mongolian-originated word) a little southeast of Tiananmen Square. The vastness of the square, and the intensity of the sunlight from a cloudless sky on a hot summer's day meant one often came from the subway tunnels leading away from the place blinking into shadow, slightly disorientated. That made the hunt for this little eatery different each time, because no matter how clear one's memory of the location of the place, it seemed always to be slightly different, concealed in a labyrinth of its own, in a corner between dark grey brick walls, one with the faintest shadow of a Mao saying inscribed upon it from decades before.

Once I got to the Liqun Roast Duck Restaurant, though, it was perpetually crowded, often with a clientele who divided almost equally between those who looked local and those who were clearly from elsewhere. The one thing all had in common was they had taken this tricky journey to find the place, and somehow succeeded, though perhaps as much by accident and chance as I. Around a tiny central courtyard with tables set outside in the middle for people to eat on, there were a few individual rooms, and a larger enclosed restaurant, where people could sit on their own or in twos and threes. The favourite drink was the local Yanjing Beer, after one of the older names of the city – large half-litre bottles, lined up on the table, with the roasted duck brought out from wood-fired ovens at the front. Everyone swore that this was the best place for the dish – although there were other places that made the same claim. Larger groups tended to end up at Quanjude Roast Duck Restaurant, which existed in a number of branches, some of them several storeys high.

But the experience at the Liqun was more intimate and the service and ambience more individual. A man who must have been the boss fascinated me by forever sitting by the doorway, looking the personification of calm despite the frenetic activity of the waiting staff and the cooks around him. Through its popularity, the restaurant showed that for many other diplomats, the day life spent in modern Beijing still left a strong desire to seek out the older, scrappier place, however hard it was to find. Maybe that was through some desire to discover the 'authentic' city – though I suspect that neither kind of place was authentic, or that both were.

Finding conducive places to eat, I came to realise, provided me with a different way of mapping the city. It was a place that had much grand and interesting architecture, but I realised the places that really attracted people were almost always connected to food – and to the story of food that the capital promoted. Here was a universe of Chinese cuisine in one space. Hearsay was the usual source of information – someone reporting from someone else, who had heard it from a friend, that a new place did amazing Sichuan, or Cantonese, or Hunan food. My own discoveries were sources of particular pleasure, something I at least owned for a little while before I passed them on to others. Along Jianguomenwai Avenue, one of the vast central arteries of the city which ran east from Tiananmen Square towards China World Hotel and then out to the roads to the seaside resort of Beidaihe and the city of Shenyang in the northeast, I tracked down a Mongolian restaurant, in an unlikely location at the back of a modern hotel. The mutton here was well roasted, and had the same texture and smell as it had when I'd eaten it on the grasslands. And while big, the restaurant tried to maintain the atmosphere of Inner Mongolia – with performers singing, toasting people, and that inevitable smell, which lingered in so many places back in Hohhot, of white liquor, and sometimes, just a tiny sting in the air of the more challenging fermented mare's milk.

Even the habits of eating were modernising, however. Fast-food joints were cropping up everywhere. It was easy for people to get by eating things that were exactly the same as they had back home. Pizza Huts were becoming common – with the salad bars a novelty that attracted customers able to build up the most improbably large structures made with walls of cucumber slices and deep foundations of grated carrot, cold potato salad and tomatoes. Noodle outlets were the local equivalent. One, bearing the name Lanzhou Lamian, was perpetually open, even in the middle of the night, and a place I could go when I had jet lag so persistent and troubling I needed to get out of bed and eat something. I had a unique experience of that dish though, because for the long trips I had taken in Xinjiang a few years before, perhaps the only thing easy to get by the side of the road when coaches or cars I was travelling in stopped were these. Having eaten them solidly for over two weeks, I had thus grown weary of their taste. The spicier noodles from the central part of China were more interesting. Atop of all of these there were much swisher chains – the Sichuan 'Southern Beauty' started to become dotted around the city, a lot of the time in the new shopping precincts, with cool, modern décor, and highly efficient service (food seemed to appear the moment it was ordered). If Beijing was often a place of bustle, business, and constant movement, restaurants and food offered an accompanying source of comfort and care. Alongside them were the swimming pools quietly instated under hotels which I used, or the spas, including a vast waterworld by a new IKEA store

further out of town which was a place of quietness inter-
jected by lapping water. Saunas were places you could just
close your eyes and recuperate, and there were different
kinds of warm water in pools that lay like a sort of aquatic
buffet, running from insufferably hot to unfeasibly cold.
These were family places, thankfully devoid of even a trace of
the seedier side of such establishments elsewhere.

In April 2003, my successor had been named, and a
return to London reared its head – the London that
colleagues talked of not as a great international city but as a
hugely expensive place where one had to revert to the harsh
life of commuting, and where reality imposed itself through
returning to what was in effect an office existence again. That
cast a pall over life in the city subjectively, and made it
perhaps more melancholy than it was in reality. I was in a
state of two minds about what was happening, knowing I had
reached the end of my time there at least for this phase,
wanting to go, but also, because of my affection for Beijing,
wanting to somehow stay. It was like trying to arrange a life
where I aimed to end up living in two places at the same
time, something that I knew was impossible, but still fanta-
sised over. On top of this was the occurrence of SARS, the
bird-carried disease that had spread in the latter part of the
year before from southern China – a few cases were now
appearing in the city. The disease itself was a kind of flu, but
it was sometimes life-threatening, and the way in which it
had spread, from chickens to humans as was finally established, was worrying. Quarantine measures were put in
place. The public spaces of the city became empty. Over late
March into April, it was not possible to meet people easily.
Friends preferred to stay at home, and few wanted to come
into the city centre. A trip to Hohhot by car meant going

through a number of checkpoints and disinfectant stations, while passing along long stretches of road that were deserted between them. I had never had an easier journey in China than this!

The whole experience, at the time and afterwards, at least gave a kind of firm termination to my Beijing time as a diplomat. And for someone who had read the great novella of Thomas Mann, *Death in Venice*, about the staying on of a writer in a city afflicted by an outbreak of public diseases, or the hugely influential work by Albert Camus, *The Plague*, what was happening in Beijing in my final weeks there was evocative, and suggestive. The place was, because of this and many other things, changing. Once I left, it would carry on changing, and at a pace faster than elsewhere. The locations I had come to know and acquire some sort of ownership over through familiarity would also transform, close, move, be renovated, or simply disappear. Some I would never have a chance to go back to. Things were always moving on, of course, not just here, but everywhere. And to be honest, so was I. I knew I would not come back here as the same person. Being an official had many good points – but I realised that most of the time, I was almost stealing opportunities to read things completely unassociated with my work. I had been doing a doctorate part-time back in the UK, and most of it had been written while living in Beijing. Being an official meant being part of a particular culture, adopting a world view that was somehow acquired, but which I kept at a distance, meaning that it was infected with issues of authenticity for me. Was this the sort of thing I believed in, and the kind of destiny I really wanted, to come back here in years' time, doing the same kind of work, though at a different level? I really wondered if I had the capacity to do this.

Beijing had taught me this time, under this guise, that there were many different options and alternatives. As a teacher, I had never thought I would get a chance to work in China as a diplomat.

As a diplomat, I wondered if I would ever return as something else – a scholar, or writer, perhaps. Because by 2003, while I was writing reviews and shorter pieces, I had not really written anything much publicly at all and had no idea writing would figure much in my future.

Over the years, as I did different things, I came back to Beijing almost like a frequent traveller. The place stayed in my bloodstream. The Beijing Olympics came and went, leaving a huge mark on both the spirit and physical layout of the city. The night the announcement had been made of its successful bidding in 2000, I remember this eruption of celebration, with firecrackers going off, and people hooting their horns in the streets. Beijing, they seemed to be saying, had arrived. The impact on the confidence of the place was tangible. And all the events, and the buildings left behind in 2008, contributed to that. Shopping centres of increasing enormity went up. Each time I came to stay, I seemed to move from hotel to hotel, some of them reminiscent of the more utilitarian places of the past, others awash with luxury and status. The ring roads increased, to five, and then six – and the underground became a much easier way of getting around the city than by taxis – just like it was in London.

In 2005, I effectively left the Foreign Office for good, after a two-year stint first dealing with Indonesia and East Timor, then an even briefer period working in a place in south London advising on UK visa policy. Being an official was always a learning experience, a way of being educated in multiple ways about diverse things. Learning about Southeast Asia had been diverting and refreshing because it involved a raft of issues that were different from those that came from dealing with China. But the idea, after successfully getting my doctorate in 2004, that I would be able to no longer deal with China was unconscionable. By 2006, I was working in a new way, partly doing consultancy on China independently, partly as an Associate at the great international affairs think tank, the Royal Institute of International Affairs at Chatham House. That meant coming to Beijing and talking to people in academia, or policy centres, and doing it in a different way than as an official. I didn't need to be so careful and cautious about what I said. Instead, I had to be creative, sometimes provocative, and write a lot, commentate a lot, speak at public events, putting together a kind of personal narrative that conveyed an attitude and a credible basis for me having the grounds to speak about my area of expertise – Northeast Asia, and in particular China.

For this work, my encounters with Beijing became more variegated and fragmented. Sometimes I would come back and speak about a book I had just written at the Bookworm Club, based near the Sanlitun bar district and the City Hotel, now no longer there, where I had first stayed in May 1991. On other occasions I would be part of think tank delegations, going into the buildings of the Chinese Academy of Social Sciences, or the Chinese Institute for Strategic Studies. Over the years, I did talks and work for *Beijing Review*, and often went to their offices in the northern area of the city, close to Beihai Park with its prominent white pagoda visible from far away. Many times, I went into the offices of companies or organisations that were keen to work with British partners, and sat around more shiny teak tables than I can count, watching briefings, discussing potential collaboration, sipping tea from cups, more often than not fighting back the impact of jet lag. As the decade wore on, into the 2010s, I would be invited to the China Radio International site, right at the end of one of the underground lines, close to the Babaoshan Cemetery, to do programmes there. And with mostly international, and sometimes Australian or European delegations, I would come to academic or official events, though now as a participant, not an organiser, and frequently as an adviser rather than convener. Some of these were held in Party buildings. One trip went into the main meeting hall of the Central Commission for Discipline and Inspection, the anti-corruption body. Another time, I was in the International Liaison Department, a part of the Communist Party in Beijing that dealt with connections with the outside world. I visited schools, went to the Central Party School in the northwest of the city, and gave talks to business people, or Chinese students, or visiting delegations. All of this was in a city where the memories of my lived experience from the period 2000 to 2003 grew a little less vivid, even though they never lost their vivacity. For me, the times when Beijing was most conducive were those very private moments when I found a specific space, a sort of area of calmness, when life could just stop for a moment – these wonderful hours when I had, while based in Inner Mongolia in the 1990s, my train ticket back to Hohhot, and was able to leave my luggage at the vast station, and simply be free to wander around the city till the train left. Or the sense while working as a diplomat later when I was in my car of being able to park somewhere not so easy to get to, and take a book and sit in a cool coffee shop or bar and read for a while, not known by anyone, largely ignored, able to experience the text I was reading while often letting my mind wander over issues till it was time to head back home. This, against all expectations, was experience of a city where life was more contemplative than full of action and transacting business. The things that survive over this period that still most matter to me are what Wordsworth in his great 'Prelude' called moments 'when I am worthy of myself'. He was talking of the profound engagement with the natural world around the Lake District as he was growing up in the eighteenth century, and its ability to awe, and inspire, the human self. For me, the personal change in Beijing was creating a space for autonomy and self-development in a city where I could either choose to be disengaged and restricted by 'otherness' or to allow some access and impact of it into my inner life. Beijing, like Hohhot, in different ways, and for different reasons, did enter that inner world, and things that happened there shaped, diversified and changed it. This city exists, therefore, as for so many other people, not just as a physical location, but as a part of me, and of my life.

SHANGHAI

上
海

First impressions of the great city of Shanghai were not good. After all, despite over six years of living in, and coming and going from China, I had never managed to make it here, to the second most important urban centre after the capital. Now, finally, I was able to visit, on what was called a familiarisation to the region after having just joined the Foreign Office in London. It was a short tour; a few days in Beijing, then one night in Shanghai, then to Guangzhou for two evenings, then back via Hong Kong to London. No more than a week all told. And the time in Shanghai was mostly spent in meetings – just sight of office walls and furniture, and the interior of the standard international hotel they had put me up in opposite the centre where the Consulate was.

There were no surprises in the lobby there, but then I asked for a small tour of the city, to finally see it. My hosts at the Consulate let me out for an hour or so – just wandering from the Portman Centre where it was based, across to the Soviet-era-inspired architecture of the Agriculture Exhibition

Hall in the late, hot afternoon, and then walking up the retail carnival that was Nanjing Lu, the equivalent of London's Oxford Street, that ran straight through the city centre. This was the time of rush hour. All of Shanghai was trying to get home. When I tried to pass from south to north of the street to get back to the Consulate, there were no gaps in the endless stream of bicycles. I had never seen so many people in one place in my life – a relentless surge, with me stuck on one side of this great tidal river of people on bikes, trying to find some way of getting across.

The city had a name as the key commercial centre of the country. It had had this before 1949, when, friends I came to know who were based long-term in Shanghai told me, foreign enterprises, visitors, and tourists came in the 1920s and 1930s, giving it an air of sophistication and mystique. It was the pearl of the Orient, a place where the actress Marlene Dietrich, the actor Charlie Chaplin, and Albert Einstein came. Shanghai had acquired an allure – a place that attracted foreign adventurers, was a home to local gangsters, and pulled in a raft of other colourful characters. One friend, the American scholar Andrew Field, even went on to produce works on the nightclub world of this era – the place where everyone mixed together in shadowy taverns and underground salons, Communists and Nationalists, Jewish and gentile – the place where, as another of my long-term resident friends there once explained to me, the world met China, and China met the world.[1]

On first encounter, it was not an easy city to conceptualise and understand for me. Far vaster than Hohhot, which had a manageability about its size even if it was different and isolated, or Beijing, where the clear, planned and regulated lines of its vast main boulevards at least gave some kind of physical structure to latch onto, Shanghai was less easy to map the shape of. Water had the greatest impact on the urban layout, and with that came a shapelessness and lack of easy regularity in terms of streets and space. Spread around a great river mouth and its tributaries, snaking around the promontory looking out to the East China Sea, with ports, one fast becoming the world's busiest, it had the trace of different communities of the past, from the French to the British Concessions, and then the transformation of this to the modern municipal areas (sixteen of them). Many of these features were there precisely due to the fact that Shanghai was built up commercially because of its proximity to oceans and seas. The pattern of this growth around the water edges and on what was once mostly marshland meant the place today has an organic feel – and while People's Square in the administrative centre offered some kind of focal point, it was initially for me the river facing the historic facades of the Bund that caught my attention and held my gaze. These great structures were the ones I found of most use in working out what Shanghai had been and was. These were where I started to build my map of the place.

The Bund buildings varied in size, age, colour, and shape. As I got to know them in my frequent visits from 2000 onwards, and as they became more familiar, their meaning changed too so that they came almost to look like different buildings than the ones I had first set eyes on. My first encounter saw them as translations from the West, and in particular from Europe, of styles and architectural idioms originating from there. They used materials like concrete and steel for the first time in Chinese buildings. But the diversity of the stories of these individual structures, and the way each one held a particular tale, meant that anyone searching for a common narrative of the Bund that united all the structures there ended up frustrated once they became a little familiar with these tales. They were colonial style, in places, but in others spoke more of local adaptations, the emergence in the early twentieth century of a Chinese iteration of modernity – a phenomenon that one saw so often elsewhere in the country and which was mentioned in its more recent manifestation in the chapter on Beijing. And in many places, they were also monuments to local collaboration with international partners, and not just with Europeans, or Americans, but Asians. The businesses the buildings had once supported – finance, insurance and banking, and, in the modern era, retail, tourism and consultancy – gave their own narrative of a city that was distinctive, unique, but also open, embracing of a world around it, and often constructed in partnership with that world.

Coming from the grand new airport built in Pudong, an hour from the centre along highways, (slightly closer on the high-speed rail that was built in the late 2000s), Shanghai's emergence is almost incremental, a slow build-up rather than some grand act of bursting on the stage in one moment. Travelling in, I usually became only slowly aware that the city was starting to occur around me along the edges of the road, until it was really finally standing right before me. The Bund was the usual culmination of many of these journeys, just seeming to happen at the end, the finale to a gradual crescendo. It was the ever-increasing number of ever-taller skyscrapers that came first, sometimes obscured by fog or clouds, and, in later years, bunched together on what had once been rural land, making them seem even more miraculous. The earliest had been the iconic Oriental Pearl Tower, but from the late 1990s it had been made less lonely by

structures like the Grand Hyatt Hotel in the Jin Mao Building, the world's highest hotel for a time (it has since been
overtaken by the Ritz Carlton in Hong Kong's International
Commerce Centre), starting on the 54th floor and then
stretching right up to the 93rd. A squarer structure, the
Shanghai World Financial Centre, vied with this from the late
2000s, with a walkway across the top which, despite being
told the glass was reinforced to such a point it was stronger
than concrete or iron, visitors often found too terrifying to
set foot on. But grandest of all was the latest arrival, the
slightly swivel-shaped Shanghai Tower, an empire of glass,
and dwindling lights as it shot upwards, its upper storeys
frequently lost in clouds above the city. One of the most
uncomfortable films on YouTube was of two Russians who
trespassed when the tower was being built, and clambered
right to the end of one of the massive cranes perched on its
top levels. Their images of the world below as a bird might
see it, only with nothing to support them were they to fall,
are enough to induce vertigo even in people of the sturdiest
disposition. Shanghai was a city that simply seemed to be
forever rising up, physically higher. Yet its history and its
success as a place of commerce were based on the tangible
fact that it was, and remained, a great port very much down
at ground level, and that things came and went through these
ports to the great markets inside and outside the country on
the surface of the earth, rather than in the clear sky.

———

From 2006, I had a reason to come to the city regularly. I was
assisting the northern English city of Liverpool, which had
been twinned with Shanghai from the mid-1990s. At first

sight, the coupling looked improbable. Liverpool, once the second city of empire in the UK, its port only exceeded by London in terms of trade and business volumes in the Victorian and pre-Second World War era, had been in decline in the post-war era. There were times when this decline seemed almost irreversible, with one famous case of a politician in the 1980s under Margaret Thatcher, the late Geoffrey Howe, simply arguing that the place should be slowly allowed to dwindle and fade away. That did not, of course, happen – it was never remotely likely it could have, or would have. But in the 1980s, after some nasty riots and huge levels of economic stagnation, the mood of the city began to transform. Reduced from a peak population of over three quarters of a million earlier in the century, it came down to just over 450,000. This was the same level as the number of new people who moved into the 640 square kilometres of the Shanghai Municipal area each year up to 2012. With 24 million people, Shanghai equated to half the population of England, let alone one of its cities. And while Shanghai by 2006 had links with sixty-six other places, spreading across the world, testifying to its global reach and the fact that everyone now seemed to want to be its friend, Liverpool's efforts were more modest. It had a handful of international partners – and Shanghai was one of the most prized of these.

But Liverpool did have things that Shanghai was interested in – culture, and football, in particular. And by the time I started to go to the city regularly, taking the two-hour journey from London, it had already been accorded the title of European Capital of Culture, at least for 2008 – and its efforts to showcase its pop music, literature, film and art achievements were paying off. Liverpool and Everton Football Clubs, though, were the real brand carriers, teams that had sizeable followings in China, and wanted to attract more people there. On top of this, the universities of Liverpool were also activists in working with the People's Republic – for students, joint research, and, in the case of the University of Liverpool, a joint venture with Xi'an Jiaotong University in the Suzhou educational park area.

Coming with a purpose to Shanghai each time, representing and attempting to transact Liverpool's business, meant I started to see the city in a new light. The place I settled on in the early years as a kind of 'home' territory was the old Astor House Hotel, opposite the Russian Consulate and near to Suzhou River. Adjacent to the Bund, and yet not quite on it, Astor House had a calm, slightly forgotten air about it once I got inside. It was not one of the scrupulously renovated massive new hotels being built – the immense Peninsula Shanghai complex, for instance, in the greatly prized end plot on the waterfront after all the other Bund buildings, which had laid dormant for years, the empty structure of the old British Consulate obscured by trees when I peeped at it through the iron grilles that bound the perimeter. From the outside, Astor House looked like a late Qing or early twentieth-century construction – grey, solid, symmetrical. Inside, it had photos lining its public hallways that testified to its historic claims. Here, they said, Mark Twain and Albert Einstein had come – with faded black-and-white images of them, perhaps during their visit. Figures from China's own modern history were present too – the premier up to 1976, Zhou Enlai, who had stayed in the hotel while active in the city in the 1930s, being amongst the most prominent. In the beige-coloured rooms, as they had been redecorated a few years before I came to stay habitually, Shanghai became quiet. The walls were thick, I was away from the main traffic, along what might also pass as a side road, and the buildings around belonged to more 'silent' trades – not businesses but a consulate on one side, and across the road, the more modernist structure of the Metropole Hotel.

Astor House had the feel of a museum in a lot of its buildings.

Wandering around it, sometimes just after I had arrived after another long flight from the UK, the dark wooden décor seemed soothing – aided by the perpetual emptiness inside the building, once one left the reception area. Along one floor there was a gallery area, with bedroom doors abutting onto it. The one time I stayed in the more ornate front rooms, it really did feel like I was in a scene from a film portraying Shanghai at its 1930s high point – ones like those the tragic, greatly admired female star of that era Ruan Lingyu had appeared in. This city had been a frontline of war in the epic Sino-Japanese battle – an urban centre where soldiers had fought each other. At that time, Astor House would have been the witness point to this, a place where perhaps people sought refuge, or they came to desperately seek relatives who had gone missing. On the ground floor, where breakfast was served, was one of the great ballrooms that Andrew Field had studied in his book on nightlife at that time mentioned above – this one an oval shape with ornate decoration around it, a place that only revisited its former glory when weddings were held here, as it seemed they often were. At the front of the hotel was a small coffee shop, a place where, when it was too hot to do much, I would sit and contemplate the easiest way to navigate the heat once I went out through the doors. Further into the building, up some stairs to the right from the café, was a bar – a place where it was dark and cool, even on the hottest day.

Taking the short walk to the Bund in the years before 2010 and the convening of the Expo, one had to cross building works, look on the area where the Peninsula was being built and over the improvements being made to the pedestrian and road areas that ran along the side of the Huangpu River between the Bund and the water's edge. At any time of the year, and pretty much at any time of the night or day, this place was full of people, the bridge over Suzhou Creek being a particularly popular place for couples to have wedding photos taken, no matter how merciless the heat on their formally dressed bodies from the sun direct above them. Here the water lapped against the walls of the jetty, sometimes made gently turbulent by vessels passing by. People may have reigned supreme on the land's edge, but on the surface of the river, it was vessels – every kind of boat or ship, tourist-laden or bearing commercial goods, vast and heaving with raw materials, or tiny and weaving between them with only signs of one or two people aboard. No river in an urban centre I had ever seen was as busy as this. London's Thames was usually empty, and placid. The Seine in Paris was dotted with small tourist boats – nothing commercial there because of the low bridges crossing the river all along the urban area. And after all, there was no port for them to go to! The Tiber in Rome was, when I stood staring at it one Christmas visit in the early 2000s, even more dead – completely bereft of any kind of movement, the water an eerie dark, as though forbidding anyone to come close to it. I couldn't think of any place, even in Asia, that was as energised from the passage of vessels as in Shanghai. That testified more vividly than anything to the life here, and captured the aspirations and hunger of the country and the city. Everything, everyone was in a rush – the future they were building had to be completed quickly, and it had to be good.

When they came to the city they were twinned with, the delegations from Liverpool that I met had responses to the place that were similar to almost every other group I brought there over the years. There was a small bar at the head of the Bund where it was easy to see how this manifested itself. I would bring the groups here because you could sit outside in the evening air, as it grew cooler, on the terrace, and be exposed to Shanghai in its night finery. Every hour, the clock of the Custom House with its small tower nearby would sound out *The East is Red*, a song from the revolutionary era, redolent of the post-1949 history of the city. At some point, as dusk was descending, almost like a massive son et lumière show, the towers ranged opposite in the place where the old Pudong area had once simply housed warehouses, fields and tracks seemed to magically burst into life. On one, a huge colourful image of a fish swimming would be interrupted by adverts for local and international watch and clothing brands. Guests I brought would settle into their chairs, if they were new to the city, holding their drinks (cold beer, or a glass of wine) and fall silent. The city played across their vision like a great performance. In many ways, that is precisely what it was – a great performance by an actor aware of their fascination and hold on those watching. This single sight was the perfect embodiment of the contradictions and the perplexities of a country run on communism but with an economy that was able to produce buildings that almost exceeded those in the West in their capitalist bravado and mercenary nature.

The view of the Bund never disappointed. And even for someone who had seen it so often, every time it seemed to tell me a different story – about the appeal the city made to people's emotions and their dreams, and about how the place so effectively married different traditions and ideas, and yet remained resolutely itself, its identity seeming to shriek from everything one saw. Looking at this panorama, I would reflect on all the different journeys I had taken over this landscape. It was a complete tableau that I was free to fill in with my own strands of experience and encounter and interaction. The gold-coloured Aurora building stood next to the Shangri-La Hotel – a place where many delegates often stayed. From here, underneath the river, ran the strange tunnel with its performances projected on the surfaces of the tunnel walls, the electric carriages taking people from one side to the other, to emerge into humid heat and light again. The Grand Hyatt Hotel, weaving its way into the sky, was where I had come once to accompany a visiting dignitary when I was an official. When I closed my eyes in the upper storeys, I could feel the building very gently sway. Or perhaps it was my imagination. Around the Oriental Pearl Tower there was a vast shopping centre, and its basement an unexpected museum of the history of the city, with mock-ups of how streets may have looked a century before. Every time I came here, I added to the accretions of sensations and impressions and recollections. But the Shanghai nightscape always had the same effect, making me become contemplative and dreamy, and helping me appreciate how hybrid and hard to categorise the city was. This was the best antidote to any temptation to adhere to an idea of wholesale difference and separation. Shanghai was so powerful as a visual sensation because of the ways in which it was familiar, and very modern, and yet very unfamiliar, because it did modernity with an energy and intensity that was different from Europe, less cautious, and sometimes almost reckless. Those skyscrapers looked so delicate and almost ready to topple with a gust of wind. But no one seemed to fear this. This was not a city to worry in.

———

My experience of Shanghai is akin to pictures at an exhibition, a series of discrete separate visits that never lasted more than a few weeks, and were usually for only a few days. I came, did the work I needed to do, then left. I never lived in the city, or was a resident there. That flavours my impressions of the place. Friends I know who did live there, some for many years, acquired a different set of experiences, something with more linearity, and less of a distance between their lives and the place. For me, Shanghai seems like a story being told to others I am overhearing. For me, I had the impediments, and privileges, of an outsider. That perhaps is the source of my particular ardour and passion for the place. Perhaps it is unrealistic, based on only brief and inevitably superficial impressions. But even so, this has continued, and intensified, for almost two decades. And as a sensation, a place to provoke and inspire, if that is all that Shanghai is to me, it has never, yet, disappointed.

Time bounds the experiences I have had in the city. I have had to be disciplined in my activities there – observe the fact that I have had trains or flights to catch, that I have needed to be moving on, never had the luxury, or perhaps indulgence, of much time. In Hohhot, time was plentiful – I could wait for things to happen, to make sense. In Beijing, it was the same. I had a commitment there, to stay at least for over three years. But in Shanghai, things had to be sought out. I had to go and find them with more urgency.

Perhaps that suits the tempo of the city, a place where one can really see the future of the China around it and the emergence of that great force, the urban-living, service-sector-working, higher-consuming Chinese middle class. Even so, I sometimes suspect, as does anyone who relates to Shanghai, that there is something I am missing, that I am looking in one direction when I should be attending to another – that there is, in effect, some vast self-deception going on, and that the reality of the place has evaded me. For instance, having been told that it was a modern settlement and had only existed for a little over 150 years, I then learned from the work of American scholar Jeffrey Wasserstrom that it had roots reaching back to the Yuan Dynasty, eight centuries before, and even before that, as a fishing settlement.[2] Having been told that it was the centre of Chinese commerce and entrepreneurship, figures like political economist Yasheng Huang showed me just how large the role of the state is in the local economy.[3] Many others were not immune to these acts of self-misinformations and buying into myths that soon evaporated. Liverpool delegates standing on the Pudong waterfront looking back to the Bund would proudly repeat the line that their own magnificent Three Graces buildings on the Mersey waterfront were the models behind these structures they saw before them. But that never made sense, as a historian of the city from the UK accompanying us once made clear. The Liverpool structures were all put up in the first decade or so of the last century. Half of the Bund already existed by then. Its most iconic buildings, too, like the vast Hong Kong and Shanghai Banking Corporation headquarters with its beautiful bronze lions positioned before it, and the cupola roof rising church-like over the rest of the structure, or the aforementioned Custom House, or even the great Cathay Hotel, or the Peace Hotel facing it, were either designed by people with no evident link or knowledge of Liverpool, or with other models clearly in their mind. Everyone seemed to want to own, or claim, this city as somehow being from them, or linked to them. Why not just let it belong to itself, I wondered. That would have been more rational, and generous – and true.

————

Lack of time in the city meant that most of my pleasurable wanderings there were accidental – cases of getting lost, or having time to fill, or simply being curious and going in a direction that I wasn't expecting when I was looking for somewhere else. Fierce heat in the daytime for much of the year meant evenings, or later in the night, were the optimal times to do this. For me, therefore, for this simple practical reason, Shanghai is a city of shadows and of nightfall, because those were often the only times when it was convenient and comfortable to move around in the open air. Such a reason is a very prosaic one. The effect, though, is pleasingly poetic. My abiding memories of the city have a sort of filmic quality, as though I were wandering around a huge film set where some romantic adventure thriller is being made. Parallel to the Bund, in the streets behind it, are the lines of less well known, and sometimes more neglected, historic buildings – the places where the set became more evocative and interesting. Encounters with the buildings here were often powerful – the rows of small businesses, ex-banks, buildings now serving as government offices. Doorways in shade led to alleyways, or into buildings that stood in darkness. Often other pedestrians who had been milling about just disappeared, and I found myself alone. Occasionally, there were unexpected sights – small dogs, the pets of people who lived nearby, running out onto the side of the road, a reminder that here too there were dwellings and inhabitants, pursued frantically by worried owners who stooped down to scoop them up (they were almost always small dogs, beautifully manicured and looked after) and carry them back to sanctuary. Other times there were courting couples, caught in a darkened corner who looked up furtively as I wandered by, and then, reassured of my harmlessness, watched me as I disappeared down the road. Shanghai, for all its energy and bustle, in these spaces so close to the very heart of the city, seemed calm and bereft of people. The most tangible reminder I ever got was the glow of neon lights reaching around the edge of street corners, a testament to how close the glorious frontage and the waves of humans on the Bund were.

Preservation of this thing called Shanghai culture and a consciousness of its uniqueness had been growing throughout the period after the city was made a special economic zone in 1991. Its natural assets that made it a great logistic hub for sea, air, road and rail were things that could be easily celebrated and promoted in the discourse that prioritised material and economic development which intensified in China from then. But it also began to appear more clearly as a historic centre, with architecture that merited preservation. Foreigners and Chinese locals worked on this together. Some of the earliest and most exemplary rejuvenation projects were joint ventures. An Australian, Michelle Garnaut, has set up the M on the Bund restaurant and

Glamour Bar on the fifth and seventh floors of the third building along the waterfront. That became a place to woo and impress people – soft interior décor, a hybrid menu that included racks of lamb, imported French wine, and the inimitable Pavlova so beloved of Down Under. The greatest attribute of the place (and it had many attributes in the years I would go there often) was that it tapped into a nostalgia for a Shanghai chic from the past, which still had viability today as the city grew wealthier again. Up on the balcony here, more luxurious than that of the small bar I took others too, I could think of what it must have been like to arrive here decades before, alighting from one of the luxury liners that plied the ocean routes between Europe, Asia and the US, dressed in tuxedos or cocktail dresses and in the middle of a journey that would take months – so long, in fact, it almost became a lifestyle. Maybe this sort of life had never existed. It almost certainly had been more gruelling than the backward view of it – but it was a nice romance to imagine oneself in, here, on the preserved platform overlooking the city laid out before one, reawakening into modernity once more.

Xintiandi District, closer to the People's Square and Park in the governmental area of Shanghai, was held up as the most extensive and successful collaboration to rejuvenate an area. In the 1990s, it had been a historic area best known because it was the location of the building that had hosted the first congress, in July 1921, of the Communist Party of China. I'd been to that museum around 2008, in the midst of writing a book about the Party, and its past, present and future. Looking at the real figures and the space where they had held their first proper meeting had made a history that seemed abstract and too large to easily conceptualise into something much more tangible and human. Outside the museum, the streets soon became dominated by restaurants, bars, cafés, and small shops. Xintiandi, the New Heaven as it translated, was preserved according to a master plan, much of it worked on by Hong Kong businessman Vincent Lo, who I met to talk about what he had intended here before, and during, the various phases of the project. He said the one abiding impression was of seeking to speak to a story of Shanghai, one that captured its unique status in Chinese history, and in being a conduit between China and the world, and that was able to balance these hard-to-reconcile things – modernity and tradition. The woods and brick facades of the shops lining the narrow streets must have appeared in the background of many films, both about the old times in the city, and also when it was a key location for political decision making and struggle in the years up to 1949. Nationalists and Communists, foreign agitators and business people, all seemed to figure in this story, and all seemed to be making a claim for their own contribution to this master narrative. During the daytime visits to the area, the place was colourful enough. At night, though, it became like a perpetual carnival, people arriving by taxi or on foot or in pedicabs, disgorging at one of the street ends before they literally fell into the paved spaces between the eateries and bars. Their nights would add to the myriad of other nights by other people who had been in this place – with the adventures, and endings and escapades that they contained.

———

The focus for Liverpool was on participation in the 2010 Expo. That was the most tangible aim that could see fruitful cooperation between the two cities. And over 2007 to 2009,

Liverpool partners put in enormous efforts to first secure a stand at the Expo, and then to make sure it was meaningful and successful. This wasn't an easy task. Back in Liverpool, on the many visits I had there, it struck me how remote Shanghai often seemed to a place that, even in the UK, felt it was not accorded the right status and attention. Liverpudlians were proud that their music, through groups like the Beatles, and their sport were globally recognised. But tourists from China who came to the city over this period were few and far between. And the Chinatown at its centre, despite being perhaps the oldest in Europe because of the port links, was also one of the smallest and lowest profile. It consisted of no more than a single street and a few side ones, with a tiny number of restaurants, some Chinese signage, an immense gate marking all of this, and everything after it an anti-climax.

Despite having occurred in Europe many times before, Expos were not something local people particularly understood. What they did appreciate, though, was the scale. Colleagues from Shanghai would come and set out their plans – talking of endless hectares either side of the Huangpu River, and of the various zones of the park they were planning which had been allocated for the event. Their projected visitor numbers were also eye watering: 70 million, more than the whole population of the UK, coming to Shanghai in the space of only half a year. If there was a chance to make a pitch and raise awareness of what Liverpool offered, this was it: the opportunity to showcase the need they had for investment, for tourists, for deeper links into a place they had been twinned with for over a decade, and with which they now had a golden chance to do something real.

Much of the work bidding and preparing for the Liverpool

involvement in the Expo was done by specialists. And as it went on, the project seemed to expand and explode. When I did go to the physical space set aside for the stand, in a former warehouse north of the river, by a tall chimney and close to the main bridge, it was hard to envisage what it would be like when finalised. There was a mock-up of a football match penalty shootout for people to play, and karaoke cubicles for those Chinese who fancied trying to mimic the Merseybeat. Back in Liverpool itself, the city rarely had the sort of buzz, even in small parts, that pervaded the air of its sister city across the other side of the world. And wandering around Liverpool coming back from meetings or dinners at night when I was visiting, I was aware of the number of properties even close to the centre that the city wanted funds to regenerate. One of the most intriguing was the vast tobacco warehouse, reportedly the world's largest brick building. Attempts to convert this to accommodation after its commercial function finished in the 1970s fell foul because of the low level of the roofs (tobacco was laid out in long strands, needing width not height) and restrictions on addressing this because the building was historic and therefore protected. (Years later, in fact, planning permission was granted, and by 2018 it seemed the site was close to being completely redeveloped.) Liverpool business people dreamed of finding commercial partners in China, to get their support in bringing some of this city's spectacular material heritage back to life. They were not just daydreaming. Beyond the Anglican cathedral, in fact, Liverpool had hugely impressive Georgian terraces – and a building, close to the station, with a palladium front and porticos – remarkable in everything except the fact it was unused and becoming derelict. There were many other remarkable buildings that merited preservation, and which in recent decades had been neglected. The most realistic option was that the two cities might collaborate in their different experiences of regeneration. That at least implied greater parity – equality of knowledge, and real sharing, rather than one teaching the other. This approach would work because they both clearly believed they had a lot to learn from each other.

Oddly, I never saw the Expo while it was formally running. My work for Liverpool ended quietly in early 2010, just before the exhibition had begun. I'd done what I could, and needed to move on. But I developed a real fondness for this British city which I had become so familiar with simply via Shanghai. That said something about the global appeal of the Chinese city. When the Expo was over, and the vast crowds had disappeared, I did work on a book on Shanghai commissioned by the Foreign Languages Press in Beijing and the local Information Office in the municipality. A large part of that was about what had been learned from the whole process of events in 2010. Of course, on many measures, the Expo had been a success – it had accommodated the crowds, and there had been a chance for over 60 million locals to see the outside world. Interviewing some of the key officials, they took me across the site. Parts of it were maintained as they had been developed for the event. The red structure of the Chinese national pavilion, of course, was still there. And so was one of the most popular of the national pavilions, the Saudi Arabian one, which was preserved as a showroom, its all-enveloping 3D ambulatory show of life in the desert still being played, reminding visitors why on some days people had queued six hours to see this.

Once the Expo had finished, the vast district it covered acquired, in parts, a ghostly look. The vacant space reminded me a bit of the parts of Liverpool that were waiting for regeneration. One large area was set aside for hotels. In 2012, when working on the Shanghai book, I was taken around to look at the blueprints for what would happen in the district. The bureau director told me of some of the challenges of hosting such a vast event, where, for instance, an immense line of toilet cubicles had been ranged. Men were easy to cater for, he said ruefully – but they had calculated on average over two minutes per visit by women, and had done everything they could to make sure there weren't endless queues. The site where the British pavilion was had been vacated early, the seeds enclosed in glass shards, which had covered the structure so distinctively, given away as gifts.

———

Part of the experience of actually writing a book about a single place was that, unlike elsewhere, I was forced to structure a narrative towards it, to divide the city up into chapter-like segments – the economic, the cultural, the historical – and try to make coherent wholes of them. One visit to interview the manager of a port facility just downriver had ended up with him saying that places like this always demanded a flow of ideas as well as goods – stock markets, insurers and assessors of risk as loads were sent out to distant parts of the world, were information-hungry businesses, and in need of capital. London and New York had become great global intellectual centres because they were primarily places where physical goods came to and fro, and these needed a financial and economic infrastructure, built on ideas, to operate successfully. Another business person, a man I had known for a number of years, whose name and personality became inextricably linked to Shanghai, told me in a café that for him the most attractive thing about the city was its futurism. It was a place where the future was happening now – in architecture, in town planning, and in the management of huge flows of wares and people. Another, an older man who had been a volunteer during the Expo, spoke about the place as one people lived in. People like him had seen the many changes and transformations over the last few decades from a much more intimate angle, as ones that had impacted on their daily lives. For these citizens, something like the Expo was a sign of recognition, a badge of pride that their city was being validated by the world around.

For the officials and the academics, and in places like Fudan or Tongji, or Shanghai Jiaotong universities, all places I had associates and friends, Shanghai figured as a strategic hub, a place, as one person close to the investment aims of the city said, that would serve as the crucible for creating a finance sector but according to Chinese needs, and with Chinese characteristics. Like in London, the stock exchange here had a virtual existence now. It was no longer a venue where people physically came to trade, to see each other's buying behaviour and plot the rise and fall of each other's wealth. That happened on millions of individual laptops spread across the country, with a myriad of private investors, watching their stocks rise or fall on their personal computer screens. One of the most energetic of these, a close friend, would literally sit in meditative silence in coffee shops, or their own home, with their computer open at a page of graphs and data, shifting their money almost constantly. That was the nature of the local market – a place of quick commitments, fast action, the need for fast responses. No wonder the future was coming here already. In some ways, it seemed the future was already in the past.

Researching and writing the book also meant listening to the views of officials, going up lifts on hot summer days to their offices in skyscrapers, sitting in formal rooms before one, two or sometimes three government workers, while they explained their area of interest. For some, the question was how to accommodate so many incomers. Tourists were easy – there were enough beds in the city on any one night now to look after people, even despite the ever-increasing flows through the two airports, and the new high-speed rail that was bringing as never before large cohorts of people from cities inland. But it was those moving to the city to seek work, or take up jobs, to stay long-term who needed attention – the new people, as these were, some from rural areas, or from other cities, and here as students, office workers, and labourers on the building sites. The city had expanded so quickly, almost doubling its population in a few years. Travelling on the elevated highway, whether towards the cities of Suzhou to the northwest, or Ningbo down south, along the impossibly lengthy bridge that ran across the estuary front, or westwards, sitting in the back of taxis, I saw the vast numbers of residential towers, densely placed in almost every direction, an army of accommodation, all of them with people living, dreaming, working, commuting on the mostly new, mostly air-conditioned, mostly extremely efficient subway system that by 2015 ranked, after Seoul and Beijing, the third largest in the world. How could one truly comprehend a city in which so many individual lives were being lived? Officials complained of the immense variations in expectations between different kinds of citizens – the new middle class, with their aspirations, their global perspectives, their hunger for a better and better life – and the migrant workers, often complete outsiders, working long hours, constructing buildings, or working in restaurants – a sort of silent presence for visitors like me, just sporadically visible as one went by building sites, or sat in restaurants. Creating cohesion and a sense of community in places where, as was true in some of the suburbs, everyone was new, everyone was from elsewhere, was not easy. Family mattered – but then I read of the tragic case of an elderly gentleman who had died in the city, and whose body had not been found for several weeks after his death. That sort of thing happened in a place where family structures were more eroded and looser, like Britain. How was it possible in a place where, after all, the extended family was the most important network of all and the most dependable one.

The book took its own shape. Part of it was an account, like in this chapter, of the meaning of the city through its architecture. This was not a place where there were ancient buildings. The Jing'an Temple, with its grand golden figure of a dragon head, was largely reconstructed. There had been no material residue from the time when the place was a fishing settlement, because then everything had been impermanent. Solid brick-built structures that were likely to survive did not appear until the nineteenth century, and then the idiom of the architecture of the outside world had already entered China and created the hybrid forms and models mentioned above. Shanghai really was like nowhere else in this respect. It was a testament to the aspirations of China going back into the final decades of the Qing Dynasty to be a modern place. But that had been a path strewn with setbacks, and dramatic peaks and troughs. The 1930s were the epitome of this, the time when the great Lu Xun and the writers around him were sharpest in their criticism of where China had come to, and how it was trying to engage with the world around it. Lu Xun's house, along with the film studios preserved as testament to the remarkable artistic fecundity of that era, was much like the quiet shrines to authors I like to visit in the UK. After all, beyond looking at the desk at which he had written, and the books he had read and absorbed information from, there was little dramatic in the lives of most creative people like this. Even someone who had lived a life as frenetic as that of Dickens, with his travelling, his epic, mesmerising public performances, and his complex private life, was hard to capture in the physical spaces where they had lived. They were not like kings or queens or grand public figures, the environment around them often suggestive and supportive of the drama of their lives and its action. They operated in a private realm – and for me as a visitor, Shanghai's private realm often seemed unknowable. It was the city of public face par excellence, the private shifted way into the background.

The simple fact is that from 1998 to today, I have never been in the private home of a local person in the city. I had visited the houses and apartments of foreigners resident – but even if they were long-term there and had inhabited the place for decades, there was still a feeling of slight impermanence about where they lived. In Hohhot and Beijing, I had visited, eaten, and even slept as a guest in local people's homes. Shanghai was not like that. It was a place of public spaces, or hotels, or offices, or meeting rooms. I was perpetually sceptical of my real ability to claim, because of this, any insight into the life of the city – and even when working on the book, it seemed to me there was this crucial voice missing, of the real Shanghai, the real resident of Shanghai, this semi-mythical figure with quick, supple thinking and worldly wise nous and self-confidence. Where did the people I met go back to at night? What were their most private worlds? They often seemed to be working all the time, like those in London, people who were perpetually in a public zone, where there was no real sense that they had another realm they retreated to in their own time.

Like in the West, too, this notion of private time, time in which one was on one's own, and able to be one's self, was almost ceaselessly under attack. Western work habits had dominated in the city. The great financial district with its dizzying modernist architecture over in Pudong area was like the square mile at the heart of the city of London, or Wall Street and the environs in New York. Vast air-conditioned, marbled lobbies in the basement of buildings that raced up into the sky were as much as one could glimpse. Occasionally, on visits where I had reason to do so, I would go into these places, hit by the cool air like a sharp spray of water, cooling down and being granted permission to proceed to one of the upper floors, for a meeting, or a talk. From the glass frontages, one could see the rest of the city, with, I was told, two thousand structures with twenty storeys or more. Sporadically, there were parks, explosions of intense green – and the snaking, busy shape of the Huangpu River and its tributaries. The décor around me though, in all of these places, was generic, only slight details would have marked it out as Chinese. It was the standard everywhere, an environment that existed in every major city on the planet – or at least, any with pretensions to be joining the global community run on iterations of capitalist principles.

Chinese life, even in living memory, had been predominantly rural. Fei Xiaotong, the great sociologist who had been trained at the London School of Economics in the 1930s before returning to China after 1949 to establish a school of sociology, had used a wonderful palette of intellectual and descriptive terms to envisage and understand this world of Chinese social relationships. In *From the Soil*, he had talked, in 1947, of a world in which communities were small, everyone knew everyone else, and the individual sat at the heart of a group of relationships, from family, to marriage partner, to business associates, one which was dominated by the concept of visibility.[4] There was nothing abstract about the world Fei described. It was one where you did business and relied on people right next to you. Their propinquity meant that if you chose to betray or let people down, then the costs were high. They were your neighbours, close friends, people who you would meet and need to deal with every day. You could not run away from them. Your misdeeds, if you committed them, would be present before you every day.

Urbanisation in China accelerated from 1978 in ways that had profound effects on the nature of Chinese physical space, but also, as with everywhere else it had happened, on the inner worlds of Chinese people, and on their interpersonal relations. Mobility increased. Millions moved from their home place to places, sometimes far away, where they worked, sometimes established families, and belonged elsewhere. Cities like Shanghai boomed, rising from 7 million people in the 1980s, to triple that figure a couple of decades later. Suddenly, relationships were not just tangible, visible – there needed to be new kinds of social bonds. Urban centres like Shanghai were the crucibles in which this new kind of Chinese world was created – one which, for the first time in history, those living in cities outnumbered those in the rural areas. That had an impact on the nature of daily life. It meant impersonal rules mattered more, new protocols needed to be established, new ideas about friendship and how to make, and maintain, friends. But it also meant that the kinds of boundaries between work and leisure that had been forged in Western societies migrated to China. There was the work life and the private life, and they occurred in different places, displaced and remote from each other, linked by acts of commuting. Farmers and rural dwellers lived where they worked. Finance workers in Shanghai may have worked tremendously hard, but they had a private life they could retreat to, on holidays, at weekends, in their home spaces, which were no longer those of the work unit model I had known in Hohhot where the government allocated spaces to live, but ones that one bought using mortgages, borrowing money from friends, getting help from networks, the new networks one had created in the renewed city.

Around Pudong in the evenings, it had the same calmness that the city of London did at the same time of day when everyone had gone home. Lights sometimes shone out in isolation in large office blocks. Someone was evidently still working, dealing with markets thousands of miles away, or finishing off some major presentation or project for the next day. People walking around, coming away from work, wore the international dress of business – suits, skirts, high-heeled shoes, ties. Conceptually, too, they spoke the same kind of language – of tending to profit and loss, or watching markets, or seizing opportunities to accrue capital. They used smartphones and computers and were dependent on many of the same apps and messaging services that others elsewhere had. Weibo and WeChat became the standard means of reaching out to people – and created, in the later times when I came to the city, the strange ritual of holding out one's phone for others to scan the barcode on it and add it to one's list of connections. Weirdly, in the virtual world, once more one was constructing a network where, in theory, one had to know, or assent, or validate someone else for them to be linked to you. And sending out a message on WeChat on arrival in Shanghai meant people who happened to be there then could reach out, see if I could meet up, tell me what they were doing. It created something akin to a private reception, a perpetual moveable feast where I was able to enter and re-enter a network of my own in the vast, perhaps infinite network, of the great city that I physically came to.

———

'We Love Shanghai' was one of the logos that appeared in glorious red colour on the Pudong skyscraper frontage when lit up at night. I could see it if I was in the Captain's Bar along the Bund perched on the rooftop terrace. With delegations, in later years – ones which I was lecturing to, teaching, informing – conveying the quality of that emotion towards the city became important.

It was like sharing a secret, a feeling of love that only now I could really talk about. And like most love, it was a little baffling, a little disorientating. In the bus from Pudong Airport into the city, on the first evening, I would tell the people on the tour that, for those who had not yet visited this place (and that was the majority), they were about to experience one of the world's great cities. They did not appreciate that: Shanghai had not enjoyed the profile it merited. People went around the world with brands on their bags announcing the places where the company was present – Milan, Paris, London, New York. Sometimes that stretched to Hong Kong.

But I didn't know why Shanghai was not more present on this material, because in many ways it was every bit the equal in atmosphere, aspiration and ambition as any other of those cities.

With each of these groups, I noticed as their own encounters with the city proceeded, that a part of that affection I had acquired over the years started to pass over to them. For me, my first visit to Shanghai had happened unaccompanied, unprepared, without someone beside me giving me any strong reason to embrace the place. Had I had that, perhaps it would have come across as less as a mass of disorganised and often overpowering sensations, and more as somewhere that was manageable, interrogable, and therefore lovable. The simple fact is that without some kind of guidance, Shanghai could be overwhelming. In the cafés and bars and restaurants and great hotels and places like the walk from Nanjing Road to the Shanghai Museum in the middle of the People's Park, I could see people become more reflective as I travelled with them. Within a day or two, they too seemed to imbibe the restless energy of the city, and become swept up in it much like the vessels on the water that were neverendingly passing by, night and day. Like novices, after the initial orientation and guidance, many of them went off to find their own Shanghai, their own particular place or discovery, a bar or a shop or a small tucked-away corner. That was where their Shanghai left mine. This was always a place for rediscovery and rediscovering, and personal appropriation. It was a big enough city to take that kind of approach.

My last few visits to Shanghai have been shorter than usual. And they have usually been characterised by a sort of reflectiveness – recollecting previous arrivals and departures from the city and the people I had met and spent time with when I was there. The Singaporean, for instance – someone who had come to the place to study for a PhD, and who had introduced me to a wholly green, sustainable (it claimed) hotel along a small backstreet, where she took me to dinner, explaining her theory of Chinese international affairs. She left. So did the British man who had become an expert on local history, writing, and giving tours of the Bund and bringing each of the buildings to life with stories of how it had come to be, how it had survived, what things had happened there, and who had stayed there. The translator, who had accompanied a delegation, and grown so weary and disengaged with their talks that she had fallen, very visibly, asleep on one of the front chairs, only to wake up when nudged and continue her portion of the simultaneous translation without missing a beat. The publisher, summoning me to a small bar where he introduced me to a colleague, an American former ship's captain whose caustic wit and relaxed manner helped pass most of the afternoon. 'My wife would know I am here,' he stated lugubriously, 'only last time I met her, she refused to give me her number.'

There were the officials from the past. Diplomats, some of whom had served in practically every part of the planet, and for whom Shanghai as the last post offered a grand finale. One of these, despite a career reaching back to the late 1960s, managed to outdrink a small group he was leading round, clear-headed enough in the final bar to win a drinking game and furnish us all with enough alcohol to send us to bed, and oblivion. Others had loftier aims. A British businessman who had set up in a small office, and who declared grand plans about how he was helping the local government redevelop one of the key sites locally, something that seemed viable until he disappeared, almost as soon as he had come, leaving debtors pursuing him as effectively as chasing smoke from a fire on a windy day. Beijing has its history and its grand buildings. Shanghai, though, above all, had its people – the world's people. For that reason, my transient, frequent visits were the best way of all perhaps to capture the mood of this city, a place that never seemed to stay still, never remained in one place – ceaseless, restless, and vibrant, and above all, profoundly human.

XI'AN

The airport is a long way out of town. That is the first clue. And if you arrive in daylight, as I often did, the landscape seen from the side of the main roads looks ancient – dry, sometimes with exposed dirt, an ancient sky looking down on an antique earth.

Bringing the Duke here was a huge endeavour. He came with an entourage – not big, but demanding. A bodyguard was one of the key members of this group. He had served as the confidante of a princess, and his tales of exploits over the years he had been in the police force filled the hours when we were driving around from venue to venue. The valet, in charge of the Duke's clothes, was quieter, sitting next to the Secretary at the back, stealing furtive looks at each other. Coming here had involved two previous trips, to look at the hotel's presidential suite, the meeting room locations, and the factories we were to visit. It was hard to see after all this due diligence how anything could possibly go wrong during the visit itself. But the Duke was not a young man. And he needed to be asleep by nine each night. That was the iron rule that shaped the activity of each day.

Being with the group meant they took up all the time. The chief adviser was an older, but more absent man – someone who had been in government service for many years, and for whom this was a final post. Following the Duke around with thick briefing packs, his main insistence beyond the 9pm curfew was to observe set times for meals each evening. Meals needed to happen by around six, no matter what. Otherwise the Duke felt put out. There was no negotiation about this.

Luckily, Xi'an city knew how to receive dignitaries. They had hosted Bill Clinton when he was president of the US. He came here around 1998, and there were pictures of him arriving at the Hyatt Hotel, a phalanx of hotel workers and the general manager, who was still there, queuing up to greet him as he got from his car. Other national leaders had come. Standing one evening while waiting for the delegation, I saw some familiar faces in these photos – the president of France; the deputy prime minister and then the prime minister of the UK; the queen of Spain; the head of the World Bank. It seemed everyone had come here. Why had I left it so long?

The Duke was here for commercial promotion. It was 2001. Xi'an had been a place of almost mythical status, almost dead centre of the country, and I had only managed to wangle a visit because it had aviation factories and that was the sector I had responsibility for in the embassy. There were two key commercial centres, both of them at that time quite a way from the city centre. I had to travel along interminable roads and pass over chaotic roundabouts, then duck into small backstreets, and along what looked like suburban industrial areas till, almost out into the countryside, the factories happened upon me. They had been moved here in the 1950s during a phase where inland areas had industrialised as a result of the threat from the Soviet Union. Going through the vast expanse of the aeroengine or the aviation factories, I could appreciate how immense the state sector was. These were the locations that specialised in the commanding heights areas of the economy and dealt with special technology, some of it in partnership from the early 1960s with Rolls Royce of the UK. Others had come since, particularly after 1978 when Reform and Opening Up meant more contact with the outside world – General Electric from the US, for instance, or Bombardier from Canada, or Embraer from Brazil. Each had joint ventures, each had a discrete area of one of the factory buildings to do their work in. To someone with no technical background like me, staring at the machinery and the various parts of the production line meant little. What most intrigued me were the structures supporting life around the industrial areas – the signs of canteens, for instance, or the workers in their uniform who passed along the peripheral edge of our vision, and the sight, in the distance, of what looked like dormitories. Further out, there were lines of apartments, much like the ones that I had inhabited in Hohhot in the medical college days, just visible on the horizon.

When we brought the Duke here, we came in a fleet of cars, one out front with red flashing lights. People gazed at us as we went by, wondering if it was someone familiar – a head of state, or a leader of an important company. The Duke, though, was far less high profile. His main interest was that, having come very early in the Reform era to China, in 1979, this was his first time back, and it seemed, from what he said when we went around not just Xi'an but Beijing and Shanghai, that he felt things had changed so much he was almost coming to a new country. Absolutely nothing had stayed the same, he said, from the way the landscape looked, to the clothes people wore, and their appearance. Sitting with his entourage in the hotel in Xi'an at night, he said how impressed he had been by a place that, on his first visit, had mostly been full of bicycles, and small, industrial lorries, and which now had roads full of cars and what looked like commercial entities all around the place.

————

To come to Xi'an was about trying to reconnect with the past, because so much of China's past is memorialised there. The city occupies an unassailable part in China's imperial histories. It was the capital during the Tang Dynasty from the seventh to the tenth century. Before even that, two millennia ago, it had been chief city of the First Emperor, Qin Shihuangdi. This was the history that I have referred to so much before – a history that was overwhelming, complex, long, varied, but which lay inextricably at the heart of Chinese identity in the modern era. It was a past that was not, and never would be, over. This history figured like a massive mountain, laying before one's final goal – trying to understand what China as a country and culture was. If I wanted to reach that goal, I had to somehow climb over, or navigate, or come to terms with, the immense structure in my way. There were no easy paths to do this. Somehow, everyone had to create in their minds a structure by which to understand this history – to make sense of it. For me, the most vivid way was to try to work out what the physical layout and meaning of modern Xi'an revealed about this history. When I took the plane, as I often did, from Beijing to the city's Xianyang Airport, I was travelling back to that past, not just to a place, trying to build up a little more knowledge, add a little more colour, to this story – the story of the Chinas that had existed before the one I was living in and understanding now.

At the heart of that was the journey, usually by car rather than bus, and certainly not by train (there were then no trains to this place), from the city centre to the district about ninety minutes from where the Terracotta Warriors site lay. There is no easy way to explain the complexity that awaited me here. The accretions of myth and reality, the ways in which the dense network of shops selling souvenirs at that time (the early 2000s – it has since been replaced by more modern, better organised, tidier outlets) was so misleading because it disorientated visits, made what visitors were about to see seem less stupendous and overwhelming than it really was, and ironically therefore even harder to process as an experience because of the extremes between what one felt at the entrance with its carnival, demotic character and what lay inside – something simply sublime. Life-size replicas of the soldiers, or small portable versions, gave the memorial an accessibility, a sort of cuddly familiarity, that it simply didn't have when I walked from the often bright and hot large forecourt before the main hall through the doors, and stood on the platform, looking down at the rows of figures, looking like they were simply emerging from the dry brown earth itself. The most powerful sight was deep down into a pit where newly unearthed figures, some of humans, some of horses, lay broken, but vivid. They too looked like they were almost life-like, and they too seemed almost as though they were fighting to come up out of muddy water to breathe air and live again.

The replica of the bronze chariot in a separate hall was often hard to see because of crowds, mostly of local Chinese, pressing themselves against the glass case surrounding this great, precious ornament – one of the most unique treasures of the world. But if I waited, if I came often enough, and stayed long enough, stationed by the edge of the dark hall, I could capture a lull in the tourists, at the start or the very end of the day, and then I could look longer, clearer, harder, at what was before me – long enough for it to start to become something real and authentic again, as though I were able to peer through this into the past from which it came, the past I had referred to above, which I was trying so hard to make sense of and tell a meaningful story about to myself.

The mystique of the museum complex was compounded by the fact that the site of the First Emperor's actual place of burial was a little to the north – and lay mostly unexcavated, a gentle mound, rising in the distance, looking unspectacular, until one knew what was below it. It was like Xanadu, a place someone had covered with a thick blanket, where there were only the faintest shapes suggesting what was underneath. Of course, it was easy to get good translations of the parts of the Grand Historian Sima Qian's history, written in the first century of the Christian era, which described the epic reign of Qin Shihuangdi, and his death and entombment. The archaeological record had supported this vast, great work's accuracy. Until the early 1970s, however, the burial site had slept. It had been mostly forgotten, until farmers and a local historian had managed to uncover the first of what would prove to be thousands of figures. Still more were being found. The tomb of the First Emperor himself, I had explained to me, was not safe to excavate with technology at the moment. Geothermal mapping had shown there was something underneath. But until there was certainty about protecting what was there, investigators had desisted. And the rivers of mercury that Sima Qian had reported, and the vast central burial site, carried on sleeping, carried on waiting, for their time of rediscovery when they would see the light of day again.

The first encounter with this site, even with preparation, was bewildering for me – too much to easily take in. Multiple visits back over the years only made the questions more manageable: the bewilderment never dissipated. There were no easy parallels, not, at least, in Europe. In the UK, structures from around the same time were mostly hill-top fortresses, like that of the great Maiden Castle, utilitarian, with more humble burial rites. The Pyramids might be comparable, but they were from earlier, and carried a different set of meanings about power and the belief system of the society they arose from. Sima Qian had given the Terracotta Warriors site figures a voice, and individuality. We knew something of the personalities, even the appearance, of the people who had been associated with this place, and had caused it to be built. They may have been buried, but they were not silent. And the faces of the warriors, when I inspected them closely, were not uniform, but each expressed a kind of individuality – the shape of their mouths, the expression on their faces, the way their eyes were open or partly closed. Even their postures varied. No two were alike.

The conclusion I carried away from the museum of the Terracotta Warriors site was always similar, no matter how different the contexts of each visit. With the Duke's group, we were granted access to the lower VIP platform. Staring from there out over the sea of figures, the impression I was overwhelmed by was of the epic quality that China had come from, and what it was as a country. Everything about the stories of the Qin Dynasty was almost superhuman – the ambitions of the state as it conquered those around it, the construction, in only a couple of decades, of vast projects that tied up manpower and resources, and which, from the vantage point of today, seemed hard to understand the utility of. Whatever else they were, they were vast tangible statements of ambition. That ambition had reoccurred in the current history of the country, the place derived from this earlier one, where the Great Leap Forward and the Reform plans had also rewritten the landscape, reordered and reinscribed it with human aspirations. The warriors and tomb were monuments to power, that was true, but they were also a vast testimony to the powers of humans, to the energy and force of their hopes, and their desire to reorder and remake the world, sometimes successfully, and sometimes recklessly. This was, despite its size, a human monument – a monument to an aspect of humanity that often came across as a little terrifying.

———

Xi'an must have been an astonishing place in its greatest and most sustained heyday, almost a millennium afterwards when the Tang Dynasty was established. For centuries, other regimes had left their marks on the landscape around the city which one could capture as one travelled around the province of Shaanxi within which it was located. Close to the airport, one of these came from the Han Dynasty, running with great longevity from the second century BCE to around the time that Rome began its long decline. It was natural to compare the two – Rome and the Han. They had a similar sense of ambition and global aim – even though most historians agreed they barely touched each other, and seemed to have occupied their own separate domains.[1]

The tiny figures of the small Han Yang Ling museum were at a site close to the airport – a nice place to visit if there was much time to fill before the plane went. They were quiet, far less visited than the main warrior area, but they were on a much more accessible and less awe-inspiring scale, and awe can often be a disruptive and uncomfortable feeling. These were domestic, playful, like the toys of a giant. There were small animals, tiny men and women, no more than a foot high, delicately carved – a more manageable way of marking a ruler's pathway with companions to whatever afterlife awaited them. And here, because there were never many crowds, I could simply sit and make the colossal effort to stare at the figures and imagine myself into the world from which they had come.

Xi'an was called Chang'an at the height of the Tang Dynasty, a period described by one scholar as the time of ancient China's cosmopolitan empire.[2] Back in Europe, I knew something about the history of this same period. Fragmented, the Holy Roman Empire was deep into its long decline, a decline chronicled by the great British historian Edward Gibbon in his magisterial classic.[3] That had been a tale marked by increasingly incompetent and tyrannical leaders, some of whom had visited shocking violence and degradations on the people they had been meant to be responsible for. For Britain, the period that led up to the fall of the Sui Dynasty and the establishment of the Tang Dynasty in the early part of the seventh century had been particularly complex and searing. After the withdrawal of the Roman protectorate in 409, the documentary record of the country simply fell silent. Only sporadic bursts of literature survived – the long complaint of St Gildas, from the mid-sixth century, with its ambiguous record perhaps claiming genocide of what were the native English then.[4] But later, archaeology had shown a more nuanced process. DNA records did not show any radical population change – more like incremental migration from northern Europe, with the base population remaining largely the same. And other sites excavated showed a complex picture, one that supported the idea of economic decline and stagnation, rather than the fiery tales from Gildas of genocide and usurpation. Cities like the one I lived close to when I was in the UK, Canterbury, simply became little better than occupied ruins, but largely through inactivity, not conquest. It was only with the return and reintroduction of Christianity that urban, civic life seemed to return, from around 600 AD onwards.

The written record over the same period in China was far more complete. And while there was dynastic turbulence between the Sui and the Tang, within a few decades the new dynasty seemed to assert an amazing level of unity over what had been historically often disparate and fractious different communities. Xi'an was at the centre of this history, the place where as many as a million people lived at this time, the end and start of trade routes that sent goods through central Asia and into the Middle East and beyond. Fragments of this time were scattered across the city centre today, inside and outside the Great City Walls which lined most of the square perimeter of the place. In Britain, one of the most impressive buildings I knew was the great and venerable ancient church at Brixworth in the central part of the country.

The walls of this wonderful monument have fragments of Roman brick, small pieces of dressed stone, which bear, it seems, burn marks and shades of scorching from possible attacks in the Viking invasions around the turn of the 1000 millennium. Brixworth somehow survived, and remained with enough fabric to be celebrated by the early twentieth-century historian of British architecture AW Clapham as 'perhaps the most imposing architectural memorial of the seventh century yet surviving north of the Alps'.[5] Recent scholarship had contested the date of construction, putting it back about 150 years. But clearly, around the time that the main buildings from the Tang were going up in Xi'an, another world away, Brixworth was being constructed. And like them, but in different ways, it preserved the memory of the age in which it was erected.[6]

In Xi'an, there were the sites around the Great Wild Goose Pagoda, a tall structure which, when I last went to it, was located by a newly built park of fountains and pavements. The pagoda itself was connected to one of the greatest of all figures in China's past, the heroic Xuanzang, wanderer in Inner Asia for over two decades, sometime prisoner, but finally transmitter of the great texts and traditions of Buddhism to China. Xuanzang's journeys were recorded on boards in the main pagoda hall. The iconography of the Buddha, and of the belief systems of this religion, were scattered around the site – a parallel to the ways in which churches in the UK were places, as some architects argued, that had to be 'read', structures dense with symbolism, and with a semiotic system that alluded to ideas about the path to the afterlife, and the kind of eternity that might await the pilgrim soul there. The symbols of Buddhism were rich in meaning, complex and rooted in diverse, hybrid, rich traditions. But for me, as an outsider, they were hard to read – something already noted in the chapter in Hohhot and my visits to the temple in the old city there. The pagoda itself was a structure full of a thick, supporting skeleton of wood. And rising up to the roof and the viewing space, one felt that for a seventh-century building, it was remarkably solid. The Buddhism temple at Nara in Japan, which I had visited some years before, was a little similar – the world's largest wooden structure, its vast hall, and epic, carved roof extending till it filled the sight of anyone who stood before it.

In the city itself, though, it was more how Xi'an's central areas preserved this sense of an ancient network of streets, and of the faint preserved boundaries of the imperial centre, long since vanished but still very vaguely preserved in a few remnants, the shape of public roads, for instance, and the memorialising of information boards that declared where things once stood. There were, as in the UK too, the clues from names – telling of gates that were no longer there, or temples that had long gone, or bells that had ceased to ring. On the walls around the city, which were as heavily preserved as the most-visited parts of the Great Wall near Beijing, the way in which Xi'an lay low within its confines (skyscrapers were banned) made it seem like a place that was resting, lying recumbent, perhaps even slumbering. In the streets themselves, when I walked them, things seemed as they did elsewhere in the country. There were the universal signs of the new China – shop fronts, often lit up bright at night, ceramic-covered buildings, and the stern, anonymous fronts of the places of officialdom. Industry had been banished to the more remote areas. The aviation and aeroengine loca-tions, mentioned above, which were an hour or so from here, was one of them. Science and technology were placed in the two special, newly established zones, both of which I had visited with separate delegations, and both of which had vast factories along roads that were solely aimed at providing access. Universities had a more central space. Founded in the 1950s, places like Xi'an Jiaotong University, or the highly regarded Xi'an University of Foreign Languages, were within walking distance of the city walls, arrived at by one of the four main entrance gates.

For builders and modernisers, the density of history, much of it unexplored, was often a hindrance and burden. Architects and developers complained that the reason they could only build an airport over ninety kilometres away was that as soon as they started to explore closer destinations, they would find something important buried in the soil and have to investigate, preserve, and give up on their original plans. The provincial Shaanxi History Museum was one of the greatest in the country – perhaps in the world – despite its demotic exterior. Many of the most remarkable finds had been sent here – for example, one of the unearthed model chariots with its passengers and eerily lifelike drivers, which stood in a room of its own, surrounded most of the time by wondering observers. There were also famous figurines of Tang Dynasty dancing women, officials, travellers, and their camels, over a thousand years old, but still looking fresh and enervated, their faces with the same frozen expressions that marked them out as different as those of the Terracotta Warriors. I went here later in the day sometimes when I was staying, and wondered when I was walking around what the place must have been like at night, with these sleeping effigies perhaps coming to life, recreating the city's human life as it was from the time they were made.

That human life went on most vibrantly in the Muslim

Quarter, set off by a square and one of the newly constructed (after much labour and avoidance of ancient finds) subway lines. The Bell Tower Hotel was here, a favourite of foreign visitors since the city first started to attract large numbers of visitors in the 1980s. Going from that to the first crowded street of the Muslim Quarter took a few minutes. Then I plunged in, usually distracted by a raft of different sales pitches, different small shops, some of them selling food-stuffs, or souvenirs, clothes, books. A friend took me on the times I came here to the Da Fa Chang dumpling restaurant, based in an old wooden shop on three floors, and almost perpetually heaving with people, even in times like mid-after-noon or later evening, when people tended to not eat. The service was peremptory. There was never enough time to waste on courtesies and niceties. But food arrived almost as soon as it was ordered, and the quality was consistently good – great trays of meat-filled dumplings, usually dipped into chilli, soya sauce or vinegar, and then, at most, a couple of side dishes. The restaurant area looked like an oasis of calm and restraint compared with the kitchens, which were usually packed with people rolling pastry, wrapping meat in it, placing trays to be steamed – it was a miracle that they managed to move at all. But the business had to be efficient. It dealt with an unfeasibly large turnover of patrons, and they seemed to be happy with what they'd eaten. I always was when I went there.

The more intriguing parts of the Muslim Quarter were not so much the mosques – they were well-interpreted build-ings I could wander around and find explanations for. The main excitement and stimulation came from small chance encounters that showed the part history played in the lives of people here even today. One was a small theatre that had an advert before it saying it was home to a 'tradition from the Qin' – that of shadow puppets. The display was in Chinese, so there were few foreigners who went to see it. But to me, the sight of cut out, delicately manoeuvred figures retelling stories that had entered the folklore of the area was intriguing. How old really were the tales, and how had they become embedded in the practices of people? The tiny business running them I came across had an air of mystery, like a film I had seen years before in Britain about a travelling fairground act where the models actually became real people. But the small figures manipulated by unseen hands and casting shadows on the blank walls behind served well as enactors of fictions on the occasion I came and sat amongst the few people in the tiny theatre space.

There were other examples of local culture that tourists could buy along the market street. The 'peasant paintings', which were becoming popular again, featured glaring primary colours, with reds and yellows in simple blocks set next to each other. They portrayed an ideal life, one that appealed to nostalgia about the countryside and its role in the regional and national history. But the simplest journey outside of the urban area revealed how complex and diverse, even in one place, this countryside was. In Baoji, a city about ninety minutes along a newly constructed highway, things were industrial, similar to any city that relied on secondary industry like manufacturing or mining. The officials I met one day with an excitable German adviser who had been locally engaged were down to earth – literally, as their main concern was exporting locally mined products. It was clear that the outside world didn't figure in a complex way to them. In Banpo, an area that was slightly closer to the town, archaeologists had discovered something even more ancient –

Neolithic remains of the earliest humans to have settled here and left traces. On the same trip, I went by the Huaqing hot spring resort, the place where famously in 1936 in the prelude before war with Japan, the Nationalist leader Chiang Kai-shek had been kidnapped and held to ransom by a group led by Zhang Xueliang (now known as the Xi'an Incident). These days, the rooms he had been held in were dank and musky with age, cool even in the high heat of summer. The complex had become a museum now, no longer used for recreation, or for people staying to enjoy the waters.

Further out from these, to the north, were the mounds under which the only female emperor in imperial times, the great Wu Zetian, was buried. There were commemorative slabs here, nothing contemporaneous with her time. But it seemed fitting, a place open to nature, where her presence was more through how she made me feel, across the long stretch of history, rather than anything too tangible or real. Empress Wu was an epic figure, regarded by some historians as ruthless and cruel, and by others as one of the most capable of all the rulers of Tang China. She had not been distracted by irrational, almost overwhelming desire in the same way that her successor, the Xuanzong Emperor, had for his consort Yang Guifei. The story of their love, and its political impact on his period in power, was one of the great tragic romances of the entire sweep of Chinese history. Their enforced separation, and her death, after the An Lushan Revolt in the middle of the eighth century that almost toppled the regime, was one of its most destructive dramas – something that carried meaning and emotion for a Chinese audience just as much as the ill-fated love affair between Heloise and Abelard in Medieval France did for many Europeans up to the modern era. Wu had been usurped, after briefly leading (hers was the only reign in this era) the Zhou Dynasty. Felled in 705, she was dead within a few months. But her impact had been considerable, one of the great exceptions of Chinese imperial history.

Because of its history, I wanted to feel that Xi'an was the most likely place where one might encounter this destination called 'Real China'. This, after all, had been the location of many of the iconic events in the history of China from deep into the distant past. Other places, like Luoyang or Kaifeng in parts of the Han Dynasty, or Nanjing at the start of the Ming Dynasty, had served as capitals of centralised states. Xi'an, though, had been the principal administrative and cultural centre for the longest time, and for the most dynasties. The Western Zhou, a thousand years BCE, was centred on the area occupied by today's city. The state of Qin, and of the First Emperor, and of a large swathe of the Western and Eastern Han, from two centuries BCE to 195 CE had been based here. For the series of shorter-lived dynasties, too, the city had served as capital over the chaotic period from the fall of the Han till the Tang's rise. And although it had not occupied this central position in the national narrative for the period after 904 when the Tang finally fell, its landscape was a collective repository, and a huge memorial in its own right to the formative centuries and millennium of what became Chinese culture, shaping everything that subsequently followed.

The great French novelist Marcel Proust had famously written about the operations of human memory, of the ways in which memories were 'secreted' in the landscapes we moved amongst and often reignited, bringing the past alive again. His greatest work, perhaps the greatest piece of fiction of the twentieth century, was *Remembrance of Things Past* – a novel I had read, somewhat uncomprehendingly, in my mid-adolescence, and then reread at the age of fifty, in a more fit position to understand its extraordinary flow of argument and complex structure. I read Proust about the same time as I was also reassessing and reengaging with Cao Xueqin's *The Story of the Stone* – and placed these great works next to each other, as cultural parallel texts, works of the utmost prestige and status in their respective cultures, that said so much about the worlds they had come from. The great area of unity between them was the ways in which they mapped social universes. Much of Proust's work consisted of renditions of interactions between people at parties, grand receptions, discussion groups. There, with subtle allusions and the almost perfect description of their dialogues into written language, he made clear the endless complexity of human communication, and of the ways in which people can express things, sometimes utterly the opposite of the surface language they were deploying. For Cao too, the core of *The Story of the Stone* is in dialogue and descriptions of people in the small courtyard buildings of Beijing, and of the ups and downs in their relationships. In very different ways, but to similar ends, Cao and Proust use language with internal referencing and contextualisation, telling stories that are different from what they appear to be at first glance on the surface.

If I took Xi'an as something like a great physical text, I found accretions of meanings in it as dense and complex as in those of the works of Proust and Cao. Some of those meanings related to the modern era, with its economic, political, and cultural symbolism and references. Others related to the world of the past, which was more submerged, either there by signification (signs from the present stating in explanatory mode what had been there before and was no longer) or reconstructed sites, meant to at least encourage the imaginative restoration in the minds of observers of what had happened before. Then there are the grand monuments that come directly from the age, with integrity and almost complete authenticity. These might be buildings, artefacts, or other objects. The question for any reader, whether of a book or something visual, or auditory, is how to interpret – how to establish some sense of a proper, honest, truthful reception of what is seen, heard, or felt.

In his essay 'Against Sainte-Beuve', Proust declared, 'Daily I attach less value to the intellect.' He goes on:

What the intellect gives us back under the name of the past is not it. In reality, as happens with the souls of the departed, in certain popular legends, each hour of our lives, as soon as it is dead, embodies itself in some material object. Unless we meet with that object it remains captive there, captive forever. We recognise it through the object, we summon it, and it is released. We may very well never meet with the object it is concealed in – or with the sensation, since relative to ourselves every object is a sensation. And so it is that there are some moments of our lives that will never be resurrected.[7]

This was the introit to his famous theory of the ways in which eating, particularly tasting petite madeleine cakes, reawoke in him these latent memories of his childhood, and of the impact of his family's love and nurturing on him. In the Sainte-Beuve essay, however, the food is buttered toast, and the giver is the cook.

Xi'an was not a place I had any ownership over in my

memory till I was already mature and grown-up. I went there from my early thirties, and my visits were, as with Shanghai, were never long-term. Indeed, unlike Shanghai, they were never more than a few days. I have never spent more than four days in the city. It has therefore been a place of fleeting encounters.

That has to be placed against the reality that its history, unlike a European or American or even Australian city, was also from a narrative and a tradition unknown to me until my twenties. I did not know that there had been dynasties like the Han, or the Tang, or the Song – nor that there had been figures like Wu Zetian, or even the First Emperor, till I started to study Chinese properly. The historical memory and the personal memory that the city embodied therefore were things I encountered and created later in my life. They do not belong to me as part of my formative memories, from a time when I was too young to have language, and in a way that was simply absorbed through my education and upbringing. They were memories formed deliberately, and which I was conscious of acquiring. I partly received and partly shaped the sense of history and my personal memory in this place. It was not shaped for me but something I had agency over, and my steps and journeys around Xi'an were parts of a very deliberative journey, in which I went to find out things, engaged in a venture of learning. That is not the way one usually acquires knowledge and memories in one's home environment. Very early in one's life, everything is more instinctive, unconscious and often passive.

The image that I had of what Xi'an offered was of something buried, vast and hidden – a history that stretched as far as the eye could see, but was also in a strange way voiceless. The warriors emerging from the brown earth were silent. The tombs were still. The words on steles were written, not said, and there was no easy voice to render them into spoken form. Over the decade in which I went to Xi'an frequently, I started to construct my own history there to lay across this massive under-history, and to at least acquire some traction or ownership over parts of the city's story. The smells and flavours when I was in the Muslim Quarter; the sights of pomegranates being sold by the side of the road when once being driven to the warrior site in an old taxi; the almost reverential silence when I stood looking at the excavated figures swirling either upwards or downwards in the pit within the Terracotta Warriors museum; the sight of the rural areas when passing through them as sorghum and sweetcorn were being harvested; and the view over new buildings I passed by at night, which stood in attendant darkness, looking over the inner core of the city, from whence there radiated more light. Xi'an, after all, was a place important not only to Chinese but world civilisation, a place that in its heyday had been the perpetual target of attack by those who wished to destroy or usurp the current order. It had rebuilt and resurrected itself over a millennium. In that sense, a thousand years after political power had left, never to return, it was a place that testified in its lively streets, in the rafts of tourists that came and went, to the science parks and signs of commerce around its peripheries, to endurance and the powers of survival.

HONG KONG

Jan Morris, the distinguished British writer (though she also describes herself as proudly Welsh, and has written about that history in her prolific works) in her memorial of Hong Kong, one of a series of books about global cities she has produced (with others on Venice and Sydney), talks of the phenomenon of arriving in the great city on China's southern coastline.[1] It is, in her account, somewhere that makes a unique impact on those who go there. Barren rock before its ceding under what the Chinese to this day call the 'unequal treaties', which granted the island to the British as a colonial enclave in perpetuity, for an air traveller descending from the skies up to the late 1990s, the excitement of coming down in Kai Tak Airport was only reinforced by the manner in which planes needed to almost zigzag between high-rise flats before arriving at the runway. The joke was always that you could almost peer into people's living rooms while landing and see what they were eating, or watching on television. With the opening of the new Chep Lap Kok Airport, further out on partly reclaimed land, in

1998, that phenomenon ended. But most other parts of the 'enigma' of arrival in Hong Kong didn't change, to coin a phrase used by the Nobel Prize-winning novelist VS Naipaul. As I took one of the distinctive red taxis along the highways into the city, coming across bridges, descending down into Central and going under the tunnel into the island, I could appreciate the density of magnificent skyscrapers, and how they almost seemed to cling precariously to escapements, in feats of miraculous balancing and juxtaposition of forces. No matter how or where I arrived in Hong Kong, I found the visual impact of that initial journey just after arriving remained the same no matter how many times I had been before.

The experience of arrival is only differentiated depending on whether one comes during the day or at night. Day means seeing the clouds that sometimes cluster over the tops of the buildings, playfully touching them, and crowding around their upper floors. It might mean seeing flashes of lightning from one of the tropical storms that sometimes whip themselves with dramatic but brief violence across the city. Often it means shielding one's eyes, even from the cool refuge of a car or a taxi, from the bright light outside. Hong Kong at night, however, is a great landscape full of visual drama. Like Shanghai's Pudong, it operates like an immense son et lumière, a play of internal and external light on the glass or metal surfaces of buildings, which, once darkness comes, almost seem to leap into a new kind of life, becoming enervated, losing the grand stillness they had assumed during the day.

My first encounter with Hong Kong was in 1991, transiting after a year in Japan as a teacher, coming to the great city in order to get, a few days later, a plane to Melbourne in

Australia to live there for a few months. I was with an American friend who had taught with me in the same prefecture. The best we could afford for our few days was a shared room in the infamous Chungking Mansions, a vast labyrinth on its ground floor of small shops, eateries, and businesses, and then, in its upper levels, basic hostels and hotels. Our room was furnished with a small fan that whirred noisily through the night. The heat was intolerable. Deep into one night, I simply went down to a McDonald's nearby to cool off in the air conditioning there, munching a burger and wanting to move on. My friend got his train tickets and visas to head north through China to Russia. I got my flight south. I did not come back to Hong Kong till later in the decade.

———

To come to Hong Kong doing business, which I briefly did in 1998 after the reversion of sovereignty in 1997, was unsettling. The impact of the Asian financial crisis had been dramatic. The city centre had an almost ghostly feel about it. The hotels seemed less busy, and the streets less animated with traffic and the comings and goings of people. Now under different administration from the last visit, the place had not changed much physically. But its atmosphere because of the economic headwinds around it was utterly different. And it was winter then, a February just after Chinese New Year, when the winds were a little cooler coming across the Star Ferry boat, heading from Wanchai to Kowloon.

As someone from Britain, a visit to Hong Kong carried a large emotional freight. It was, had been for over a hundred years, the place where business people, academics and journalists came to know more about China over the border, even in the years when it was hard to physically get into the country. China watchers, if they were based anywhere at this time, were based here. Many of them I grew to know as I progressed in my career dealing with China – people like John Gittings, the fine writer and journalist, whose books I had learned so much from when studying Chinese in London, and who had been Hong Kong-based in the 1960s and some of the 1970s. Some had even longer pedigree. The legendary Clare Hollingworth was a British reporter who had been the first to witness, and then broadcast to the world, the hostile intent of Hitler when, on a chance car ride while in Poland, she had seen tanks of the German army massed along the border ready to move in September 1939. She was based in Hong Kong for the final decades of her life (she died at the age of 105 in 2017). While I never met her, I knew of people who spoke of her from personal experience, in awe of both her longevity and formidable character. Her table at the Foreign Correspondents Club was still set, though unoccupied during her years of immobility due to great old age.

Hong Kong as a vantage spot, a place for gaining knowledge about China, Chinese language, Chinese culture, made sense. But it hadn't been the school that I went to – that was in the north of China, in Hohhot. My experience of the Mainland had been direct. And that had given me a different perspective, one in which the Hong Kong-nurtured British view of China was slightly alien to someone like me. We belonged, in a sense, to two separate cultures of Chinese observation and experience.

Empire, after all, was an increasingly heavy and ambiguous burden, and one that had grown more contentious amongst historians. Some, like the Scottish scholar Niall Ferguson, had argued plaintively that the empire had been a force for more good than harm, an early precursor of imperialism, setting out global rules and norms, that were then implanted elsewhere, enabling common discourse and trade.[2] But there were plenty of others who attended more to the violence, injustice, and deep racial divisions that colonialism created. On the whole, I was more sympathetic to the latter argument. To me, empire was an issue for a country that existed before I was born. My Britain occupied a different space in the world – one in which it existed due to a set of alliances with other powers where cooperation and mutual respect were the new normal, not aims for hegemony. That was the ideal at least.

The hybridity of Hong Kong, therefore, was fascinating to someone with my background, but also a source of unease. This was not about the way the city managed to combine different communities and accommodate them within its space. It was more about the impact of being in this sort of environment for me, and how its colonial and Chinese aspects left me uneasy and slightly divided. Hong Kong had been a place that was familiar even before I had had much awareness of China at all, simply because of its historic links with the UK. When I was small, the first foreign cuisine from outside Europe I had really experienced had been from the city – small restaurants opened up in the UK from the 1950s onwards as people came to settle in the UK. This food, I came to know, was not so much Chinese food, as Cantonese, an important subset, but as distinctive as Italian cooking in Europe is from, say, Greek or Swedish. People of Chinese ethnicity I met before my mid-twenties were overwhelmingly either from Hong Kong and from families that had originated from there. And what little of Chinese culture appeared on British TV or in cinema was from the city – the most visible being the works of the great Bruce Lee, a massive and popular figure through his Kung Fu films in the early 1970s, before his tragic, early death in 1973. Hong Kong, to all intents and purposes, for a British person at primary school in this period, was China. Photos of the city, images on film and in literature typified how they thought the Chinese world was.

British engagement with Hong Kong was another matter, a different subsidiary community. It involved mostly those connected with the colonial government in the city and its support networks back in London, or with business. These contained groups that had defined links with the city, and seemed to belong to a particular well-defined specialist universe. Mostly their membership was made up of figures who carried a certain air of privilege for me – people who had the exotic luxury of having family or lives abroad, as well as those who lived in Britain. After school, this conviction grew even stronger. At Cambridge, for someone from a state grammar school, the dominance in the 1980s of those who had gone to fee-paying schools, and in particular to a small group of the oldest and best known like Eton or Winchester, meant that I was hit with a tangibility by the residue of the British class system I had never really experienced before. And it was likely that many of those who were British and had any links with Hong Kong would be from backgrounds like this – relatives of those who worked in the colonial administration or the Foreign Office, or in banking, or in business, where Hong Kong figured. Of course, this did not account for all the British links with the city. There were plenty who had been police there, or worked for the army. But it seemed to account for a high number of those I met.

In the apex of Thatcherism in the 1980s, where making

more and more money seemed the guiding obsession for many people, Hong Kong existed as a place where people with the right connections could go and pursue business careers, living lives that were often almost utterly divorced from the community around them. Some people I spoke to based in the city later in the decade, long before I even started considering working on China, gave me the impression that Hong Kong was a place that just happened to have people of Chinese ethnicity living there. For them, it was a whirlwind of parties, social engagements, hanging out with people from the UK, the US, or elsewhere, where the only real engagement with the city's local population was almost accidental. Christopher New, in one of the finest literary renditions of Hong Kong, a trilogy he wrote in the 1980s and 1990s, described this well – a sort of stage on which foreigners and Hong Kongese wandered by each other, occupying different levels of the same space, coexisting but rarely cohabiting or sharing.[3]

That was changing of course. But it fascinated me as I became more familiar with the Chinese world from the 1990s onwards, and lived in China more, how there really did seem to be a sort of 'British Hong Kong based' view – and one that differed from it, where my own views seemed to fall. The possibility of a privileged space for being foreign for those who wanted it, after all, existed in both environments. But in Hong Kong it was better established. In China, there were barriers that impeded this excluding option and made it less straightforward. The place was too big and complex to create a life there that existed untouched by what was going on around one. Whatever walls there might have been were porous, in ways which were not so in Hong Kong where for much of the time before 1997 it seemed one really could ringfence one's life so that it occurred mostly in luxury apartments, chauffeur-driven cars, and social and work environments where local Hong Kongese were anonymous presences, figuring either as servants in some capacity, or carefully selected individuals given a special right of entry. That seemed a strange situation to me, because I was always very curious, and these sort of boundaries or walls immediately started off a raft of questions for me: What was the other side? Who were the people living there? What were they doing? What did they think of this situation? I had this curiosity wherever I went about local life, whether it was in Europe or elsewhere in Asia. The only difference was that at least in Hong Kong or China I had the language skills to make connections and find out answers to questions I had. (I should stress though that of course there were plenty of non-Hong Kongese, and many from Britain, who did bridge that divide. They just never seemed to be in the majority.)

———

Seen in the right kind of weather, with low lying mist, from one of the islands that constitutes the Special Administrative Region (SAR), as it now is, Hong Kong has an almost floating, mirage-like quality. That is a phrase used by some who have written about and researched the city – the ways in which its great skyscrapers rise as though from nothing, each with its distinctive personality.

The most iconic are now the Bank of China building, and the idiosyncratic Jardine Matheson headquarters, with its round porthole windows, overlooking the Star Ferry terminus. One can weave between these buildings on the walkways and covered pedestrian passages, starting from Hong

Kong on the island, overshadowed by the hills on one side as they rise up steeply to the Peak, and on the other by the grand hotels like the Shangri-La or the Conrad. In the periods of strongest heat, in July or August, when even a few moments outside can leave your body dripping with sweat, travelling across the city via these passageways, going into and out of air-conditioned buildings, becomes a means of survival – moments in transition outside, when the heat licks at the body as it moves swiftly along, and then those abrupt entrances, usually via automatic opening doors, to the icy tentacles of the interior environment. Pacific Place operates like a swimming pool of air in this journey, a huge continuous exposure to coolness before having to duck out again along the elevated walkway over towards Wanchai, parts of it descending to street level. Before too long I had a survivors map of these routes in my head and could have walked them blindfolded.

My stays in Hong Kong were marked by the kind of hotels I found myself living in each time. I never again had the pleasure of surviving in one of the simple, hot rooms in the Chungking Mansions, and in my subsequent visits to Hong Kong the most I ever saw of this building was from the outside, stunned and impressed by its ability to maintain an appearance of almost perpetual grimy disharmony while the world around seemed to be forever trying to gentrify and beautify itself. Business hotels in the New Territories were the favoured stopping place in the brief two years I was doing business – chosen for convenience and economy, and rarely having much more than a basic restaurant and a room that was indistinguishable from functional rooms across the face of the rest of the planet in places like this – a base just to try, even with harrying jet lag, to sleep.

As a diplomat, though, the main accommodation was the Conrad Hotel, simply because it was almost literally across the street from the British Consulate General, a grand stone building that sat at the base of the first steep rises to the Peak. The Conrad had an air of extraordinary calm and luxury, despite the fact that it was only one of several five-star residences in the area. What impressed me most about it was the stillness in the rooms, the way in which one never heard anything even from neighbours, and how, when the curtains were opened on the sheer plate glass windows, one looked across to a Hong Kong, depending on the direction one's room was pointing in, which lay like a tableau infected by the same stillness outside as within. Down among the streets, of course, the city was perpetually moving. But from high above, it looked to be immobile, silent, frozen. There were times when I could see birds soar above the city from these windows, floating around, their wings outstretched, weaving their way in majestic swoops down to the streets below before suddenly jolting up and rapidly ascending again.

It was the dark wood and the dark carpets that contributed to this hushed, tranquil air the hotel had. Their subdued colours seemed to dampen everything around them. And after all, as temporary homes, hotels are important – places one must quickly feel secure and comfortable in, so however this sense of tranquillity was created, it was very welcome and necessary. On the seventh floor, if I remember correctly, there was an even larger frontage of glass, and I could sit in front of it, alone or with friends, as the day ended and darkness came on, and see the city light up, the glow of the neon lights colouring the air with a yellowy-orange tinge. The bar here gave the impression that somehow the whole city was a kind of personal living room. It had that closeness and intimacy.

There were plenty of other places to lap up luxury – the Shangri-La, only next door, and the JW Marriott a little down the street. On separate visits, I came to all of them. Some were for Foreign Office business, though none of it high level, or remotely resembling the atmospheric novels of intrigue and espionage that were written by John Le Carré. At most I was trying to promote aviation and airport trade, the sector I was responsible for while in Beijing. At other times, I was in the city to attend events. One was to speak at the CLSA brokerage firm annual conference, a massive investment promotion gathering where, on one night, the American singer Mariah Carey performed for the delegates, nearly flattening the Hong Kong convention centre with her powerful voice. Another was the local literary festival, held in the autumn, where the hotel was further along the island, crowded with people trying to promote their novels, poems or non-fiction works. I came here to speak about the first non-academic book I wrote, *Struggling Giant*, a brief overview of where China might go in the twenty-first century.[4] The launch event was held as part of a panel in the boardroom of a business further into the city. A year or so later, now at Chatham House in London, embarking on a career in the world of international relations think tanks, I was writing a report on volunteering, for the UN Development Programme, and came down to the city to meet some academics. That time, I stayed in Tsim Sha Tsui, in a Langham Hotel that will forever be unforgettable because of the smell of roses in the air inside, and the quietness of the rooms despite the chaotic situation on the streets outside, which happened to be right next to a marketplace.

There were other places. But what differentiated them was often the quality, if they had them, of their swimming pools. It was there, early or late in the day, depending on what I was doing, that I tried to get some exercise, doing as many lengths as I could between children of other guests playing in the water, or other adult swimmers going faster or slower than me. The pool at the Shangri-La was excellent, of course – outside, with the sheer walls of the hotel towering up so that if I lay doing backstroke, I could gaze up at the windows, reaching into the sky. The pool at the JW Marriott over in Wanchai was larger, and as light faded, it acquired this almost ethereal quality, candle-like lights around the oval edges of the pool, highlighting bamboo plants, and the occasional stone statues of serene Buddhas, brought to life by the play of light reflected from water across their surfaces. In the cool water, passing up and down the pool, being immersed, sometimes unable to hear anything, the city seemed friendliest of all – a place of conviviality, of meeting friends later in the evening, and, as we once did, drinking in the small bar by the water as lightning and thunder rolled over the earth, and sent stabs of charged electric energy down so that they lit up the hills around and cast their image across the ruffled surface of the water.

Sitting in the tranquillity of a hotel room high up as a typhoon came on was dramatic – but it didn't take much imagination to think of just how terrifying it could be, being outside, in a plane, or on a boat, as the winds grew stronger. The times when I was sitting in planes waiting to head off when strong winds were coming on and I could see flashes of lightning in the distance, seeming to grow ever closer, were always unsettling, no matter how often I flew. In fact, the more I flew, the more these occasions worried me, in a perverse inversion of what one could expect. I knew the statistics about the extreme unlikelihood of anything happening. And I knew it was more likely that an accident would happen crossing a simple town street than sitting in the skies in a modern plane. But the drama in the skies, and the implicit violence of a thunderstorm, always created emotions that were hard to reign in. They brought back memories of storms when I was younger, and of the old idea that this was down to giants from some mythical land shifting around furniture in the sky above. Maybe as I got off the ground from the runway and reached into the skies, maybe as the plane came through the cloud cover, over Hong Kong I would see from within the fragile interior, gargantuan airborne figures, like gods from Chinese mythology, clashing with each other, creating the sounds and flashes that were visible from earth. The sky more often than not, however, when I was high up above the city, was dark, except for the worrying slash of brief, intense light, before that faded, and I got deeper into the journey to wherever the plane was going.

———

Hong Kong is a political place for a British person – a landscape that is mostly human, despite the natural setting, where the water all around is incidental to what humans have built and nurtured here over almost two centuries. As a political place, part of its landscape and the built environment testifies to a prior and current order – the colonial style, older buildings, those like the Government House, white and delicate, in amongst trees. There is the Hong Kong Club, now in a modern building, and the various older buildings, like churches, or university administrative or teaching buildings, that are dotted around the city. The clock by the Star Ferry terminus has an iconic status, as does the Peninsula Hotel, standing close by. The politics of this old order sometimes manifests itself in statues, memorial stones, and in many of the tombs in the Wo Hop Shek public cemetery that sits on a hill in the New Territories.

The new order was in the buildings where finance and commerce and the new administration of the city were conducted. These spaces were more anonymous, less easy to interpret, similar in many ways to those that existed throughout the rest of the world. The most symbolic for me were the Independent Commission Against Corruption (ICAC), and its offices on the island, and the stock exchange. I was shown around both of them as a guest of government on a special tour in 2015. Based in Sydney, the Hong Kong SAR representative there had kindly invited me on a week-long study tour of the city, talking to officials, administrators, and going to housing commissions and other projects. The ICAC meeting paralleled one I had been on at the Central Commission of Discipline and Inspection in Beijing only a year before that. But here the reception room was smaller, and there was a museum tucked away on the top floor explaining how the ICAC had ended up being created. Photos from the early 1970s commemorated one of the most infamous cases, of a policeman originally from Britain, Peter Gobder, who had absconded from the city despite enjoying a successful career there because of hundreds of thousands of dollars of kickbacks he had been taking from local business people in protection racket money. After extradition, Gobder had served time in Hong Kong's jails amongst some of the very people his work had been instrumental in putting there, before fading quickly into obscurity after his release. His

Wikipedia entry currently (as of July 2018) suggests that he is still alive – aged 96, though information about his whereabouts is sparse.

While the ICAC building exuded calm, efficient authority, its corridors largely quiet and empty, those working there no doubt immersed in confidentiality and secrecy, the other place that was iconic, the Hong Kong Stock Exchange in Exchange Square, was a place where I almost expected the opposite. In fact, it was even more silent. Symbolic of the city's greatest prowess and source of influence internationally – its world class finance sector – the space allocated to the trading floor now was uniformly quiet. A guide who showed me round explained that since computerisation a couple of decades before, the room, once full of traders frantically doing deals and signalling to each other to buy or sell, was now occupied by banks of screens mostly with their surfaces dark, and a large display above showing in bright graphs the rise and fall of particular company stocks. There was simply no one here to see this though – other than hotel rooms, the place was the quietest in the city, an oasis of calm and tranquillity. It was odd to think of how much drama occurred here under this veneer of peacefulness and inactivity – mostly through the screens and on the smartphones of shareholders and their representatives across the whole city and further afield.

Seeing the reality of Hong Kong under whatever political attitude or map one brings to it is difficult. In my early visits, the lazy assumption I made was just that the place was one typified by wealth. That, after all, was the declaration that the great buildings along the water's edge seemed to make. It was behind the story, told to me so often it became a cliché, that the most Rolls Royces in any one place were those parked in the Hong Kong Jockey Club car park. Hong Kong was where, frequently, on global league tables, property was the most expensive, and the cost of living was the highest. And from the moment I arrived, from the airport to the hotel, it seemed wealth was the message I was getting – that this was a prosperous place, a place of business, the creation of riches, the fulfilment of dreams. What else, for the most part, were those British who came to the city in the last decades, joined by many other expats afterwards, searching for, but to be part of this great venture?

And once more, it was hard to peer beyond that display, and to be more sceptical about what sort of message the city landscape was really sending. One of the many platitudes about Hong Kong is that it is a place of passivity, a cultural desert, where the only things that matter are shopping, eating and working. Like most platitudes, there is a dose of truth at its heart. Wandering from the excellent underground up at street level, when the weather permitted, I realised that Hong Kong was not a place I ever went hunting for particular museums or old buildings. There were no grand galleries like the Louvre, the Prado, or the British Museum. Nor was there anything like a comprehensive museum of local history. Instead, I had to treat the place I was walking around as what was on display. It was its own gallery and museum. And a large part of that was the vast number of places devoted to eating – from the tiny snack bars huddled at street level owned by families or sole traders, to the more modern, air-conditioned chains, to the grand institutions boldly boasting of their Michelin stars or international accreditations. Nor was all of this Cantonese, or even Chinese, cuisine. Hong Kong had its fair share of Indian, French, Italian and Japanese offerings, some of them utterly superb. And it boasted, and excelled, at seafood. On its food alone, the city could claim a global ranking. And the commercial organisations, banks, businesses, cars whizzing to and fro with people in suits in them, and numbers of people walking, eating, talking, with their smartphones either pinned to their ear or relaying conversations with earpieces, showed this was a place where there were plenty of people working – and working almost every hour of their waking lives.

Despite that, little by little as the years went on and I went to the city more, the almost monolithic façade of wealth and riches, conveyed by luxury shop windows with their handbags and designer dresses and jewellery, started to be replaced by a more nuanced, complex narrative – one in which, through different journeys, I would see what life was like for many people who lived there. For them, costs were high, competition for space fierce, and pressures to maintain a good standard of living as unrelenting as they were in Shanghai, London, New York, or any other global centre like that. There was no such thing as easy money in Hong Kong – not for the vast majority of people. Lodging near the Chinese University one winter, after attending a conference there, I walked down the hill from the main campus and realised that those people working in the offices and shops and restaurants in the famous city centre often had to come from suburbs spread out to the north into the New Territories. People who had lived here for decades, like the former journalist, administrator and now academic Leo Goodstadt, had written of the less well-known aspect of the city – a place that was not there solely to look good and appear affluent, but one where the rest of the people had to live harder, more humdrum, and often unknown lives.[5]

That always lent a certain tension to my response to Hong

Kong. I carried with me those responses and imaginations towards the city that were largely gained from filmic, literary or cultural representations of it, and were often very specific to the UK and its unique experiences here. For me, Hong Kong, when I first came in 1991, had the air of somewhere that was about to undergo momentous change – and where an encounter with the People's Republic through reversion of sovereignty after 1997 was about to remove barriers that had been there for over a century and a half. No one quite knew how this would proceed – with tension and speculation often dominating conversations up to the moment when the hand-back became a reality in mid-1997. The Hong Kong of my first memory is therefore literally another place – a place best typified by a visit, one blazing hot afternoon in August 1991, to a subterranean bar to cool off, where a fellow Briton, working there for his holidays from the UK, was nursing a terrible hangover, serving my American friend and I a couple of beers with a look of sour misgiving. He said, almost world-weary, that he was preparing to leave. We too were simply in quick transit. There was no time to try to make any more meaningful emotional bond with the place.

Decades later, during longer stays, I kept on being haunted by this city that had existed in the late era of UK rule – a place where so many of the people I worked with at the Foreign Office had been involved and active. For a whole cadre, being part of the negotiations over the handback of Hong Kong was part of their collective memory, of their shared experience. For many it had been the backbone of their career, something that had defined their professional lives. But I had joined after all of this had ended, in a period as it were of simple retrenchment and tidying up. It was like arriving at some enormous conference after the final session is over and seeing the chairs and lecterns being packed away, the attendees leaving, and the session papers being boxed up and disposed of.

However, the Hong Kong that had existed before 1997 proved hard to avoid. It was spoken of often by people who had been there – mostly British expats, but others too, and was present significantly as part of my own imagination for what the city was like – a place of observation, a vantage place as it were, in which people came, immersing themselves in the neutrality of the city, and sometimes simply waiting to move across into China, something I have referred to above. This city had a distinctiveness about it, an air of nostalgia, something captured in the creature comforts that rained down on someone when they went to stay at a nice hotel, or the fact that, in the early years at least, while working in Hohhot, it was to Hong Kong that colleagues disappeared in order to get stocks of food, or goods, or experiences that they could not find easily back in China itself.

That elusive air of a Hong Kong where the past is still faintly present can be captured, for me at least, in those small signs that make it unique – the green and red taxis, the street signs in English and Chinese with their memorialisation of figures from the British era in some cases, the calm, faded comfort of the Foreign Correspondents Club, or the ways in which one can still find places of relatively untouched nature on some of the islands that constitute the whole region now.

One of the most evocative journeys I made into that more natural Hong Kong was towards the end of the 2000s, after I'd been travelling for almost a whole month around China itself. From Beijing, where a torrential deluge one night had awoken me from my sleep, to Hohhot, where I'd witnessed first-hand the epic changes in the place observed in the first chapter, to Shanghai, Xi'an and then Chongqing, I had finally made it to Hong Kong, and needed to speak to a couple of academics before heading back via Shenzhen Airport into the Mainland again. They lived in a house on Lantau Island – somewhere, they told me, they had just bought. It was easy to get to by ferry and then on foot, even with the cases I was saddled with.

The journey across the water was easy. I had made these sort of forays to Zhuhai, and Macau – travelling up to an hour on boats of various sizes, often enjoying the breeze, and fighting, occasionally, against the brief stabs of seasickness that disrupted my calm. Lantau was a pleasant bay to land in, with a few quiet restaurants, at least that day, and then a small path where my host led me to their house. For a few hours we sat talking there. And then he called a taxi, and told me of a route I could get from there direct to the Hong Kong airport, and the bus stop from there over the border to Shenzhen.

The taxi journey was a revelation – along snaking roads, often very narrow, with mostly woods banked at their sides. Nor were there many other cars around. This was truly a place one could imagine retreating to, secluded, still and quiet. Even the skyscrapers around the bay disappeared. At some points, all I saw were the road, the trees beside and the sky above. Eventually, the grand modernist shapes of Chep Lap Kok Airport came into view, and then the arrival lobby, and the rush to find the proper bus stop for the cross-border service to Shenzhen. Time was running out. I had cut things ridiculously fine. I worried all the way to the passport control, desperate that we would get through quickly, then when I finally got to the other side, I grabbed another taxi and urged the driver to get to the airport as quickly as possible. I made it, but with minutes to spare.

There were other routes to leave Hong Kong – by train, up to Shenzhen was a common one – but of course it was usually by flight. And as the years have gone on, of course, the city has changed – the place where I arrive and leave each time is modified, physically as well as in its atmosphere. The smells of the small streets and their different kinds of foods around Wanchai and up further into Central, though, and the sounds of the city, maintain something distinctive, and that is still wrapped up in this very specific memory of what Hong Kong was for me over the years I came to it. This is not the attitude, for instance, of those who, for different reasons and from different backgrounds, lived there long-term. Nor is it perhaps the kind of feeling that another visitor who has been there many times might have. For me, though, Hong Kong grants everyone the ability to make something unique of the smells, the sights, and the feelings of the place, and to read its landscape in a manner that suits them. That, more than anything else, remains unchanging.

EMPIRE OF THE SENSES
AFTERWORD

Roland Barthes, the great French philosopher, talked of Asia, for someone from a European background like him, often being an empire of signs.[1] From the status of Chinese characters, and the ways these figure in the writing systems of others, to the iconography on the landscape, the meaning given to statues, and features on buildings, even the way the natural world seemed to be arranged, everything seemed to give itself to interpretation. He admired the aesthetics of Japanese gardens, with their meticulously swept stones and the flower arrangements that sometimes dominated their central areas, because these indicated a sense of Zen-like nothingness and calm. They had great symbolic import.

For me, China is an empire of senses – a place that in the end makes as much a sensual as a cultural or intellectual impression. Its streets and public places and restaurants and shops, look, smell, feel different – different from each other, and different from what I had been familiar with in my 'BC' life – my life, up to the age of 24, 'before China'. The issue was how to assimilate and make this difference 'familiar',

how to own it with any authenticity, and how to finally live in a way in which one avoided a bipolar existence, as referred to above, but had some kind of valid boundary between the two realms – that of the life in, and dealing with China, and that of the lives elsewhere.

In the Musée de Cluny in the fifth arrondissement in central Paris is the great tapestry, anonymously made perhaps five centuries or more before, of the Lady and the Unicorn. The museum itself is on the site where there were once Roman baths, and parts of these are still preserved. Cool even during the hottest day, the rooms are full of statues, frescoes, stone masonry from the Middle Ages, the period that the exhibition focusses on. For all the diversity in this collection, what is striking is the shared imagery, a vocabulary connected with the Christian world view that dominated during this era, and the ways in which it created a set of images and their associated meanings. These crept into almost every piece of art or artefact presented in the Cluny.

The Lady and the Unicorn, however, with its six separate tapestries hung on the wall, is different. Its symbols are not those of the standard Christian vocabulary. They are clearly about love and desire, and the lady stands in the midst of a world in which she objectifies desirability, and figures as an ideal. She is clearly more than just a physical being. The unicorn, a mythical beast, prances around her, as does a small monkey and other tiny creatures secreted in amongst the foliage and the colourful background. The room in which the tapestry hangs is darkened to preserve the delicate material, and that darkness makes people fall silent. It feels like a shrine, not to a God, or gods, but a set of feelings the tapestry represents. Courtly love was the tradition this piece speaks to, and arose from – a set of noble practices and ambitions that reached their peak in literature and art in the fourteenth to fifteenth century. But as the explanatory material for the tapestries makes clear, the real meaning of the pieces, if there is such a thing, is shrouded in mystery. They are just incredibly beautiful and suggestive, and on my visits to the museum, I would sometimes sit for hours in front of them, simply trying to absorb what they portrayed, but also trying to allow a meaning from them to emerge, a meaning for me at least.

The easiest story of this great masterpiece is that of renunciation, and of senses – of sight, taste, touch, hearing, and smell. Mirrors, musical instruments and food are all arrayed in specific tableau depending on the sense being imagined. The final picture is of a tent within which the lady emerges, with 'To My Sole Desire' inscribed above.

What would China look like to me, not just according to the five places I have attempted to describe here, but to the five senses? If I think of the country and my many experiences living, travelling, and working within it, what kind of world do I get? What image of China can I create? When I am there, it is a place where I am immersed, not just intellectually, but also in terms of its impact on my eyes, my ears, my nose, my hands, and my taste buds. If I attend to these, and try to synthesise them, what kind of a place do I see?

China is, of course, a territory that makes a tremendous visual impression. It looks distinctive – even from photos of great scenes, some of them written about in this book. The Great Wall, the Terracotta Warriors, the mountains of Guilin, the Pudong area of Shanghai – they are now global icons, carriers of the image of what China is, partially communicating its diversity just by the way they look, and the way that look is different. But to me, what was more striking was the colours of places in China, and the variations of the natural light. The great portraiture painter Lucien Freud, when asked why he had remained based in the UK for most of his career, answered simply, 'Because of the quality of the light.' And it is true – the light in Britain when the skies are clear, or even when they are overcast, has a specific quality, slightly different from that of the nearby Netherlands, or the northern area of France, which always seems slightly duller, or slightly less varied.

For me, China's light was stark and blue and bright in Hohhot, usually because there were seldom many clouds in the sky, at least in the summer months. In winter, it became a little dimmer, and there was always the impact of smogs. But it was different from the light in Xi'an, which was dimmer, weaker, and seemed to come from a more ancient source, almost as though it had aged as the city it spread over grew more antique. This light could be bright too, but in the winter, when it reached below zero degrees, it was usually quite uniform, like it came from a great lamp in the sky kept on a particular setting. Shanghai's light was more from the buildings when evening came on, the dazzling displays that played across the glass fronts of human-made structures, not something natural but created. In Beijing, it was the light of autumn, when the heat decreased, and the outside world became less fierce to go into; this light brought a sort of intimation of comfort and quietness, the light of private moments in gardens or quiet spots in hotels, sitting and reading while the world hummed on around one, and things seemed to slowly settle down to rest, for night. Hong Kong's light was more variable, subject to the great clouds that soared above, and sometimes blocked out the sun, or scuttled when great storms started to appear. It was the epitome of drama when, as I sometimes did, I stood on the bayfront and could watch what the clouds were doing and how they impacted on the light. Things looked a certain way, for sure – the Great Wall, the Forbidden City, the Oriental Pearl Tower, or the Bank of China skyscraper in Hong Kong; they had their outlines and their distinctive colours, and their contours. But the light in which they stood, the Chinese light, also had an impact on them – and there were many times when that was different from the light I had known elsewhere.

For sounds, it was the same. The call of the milkman coming around each evening in Hohhot, hauling his two large canisters of freshly produced milk, crying so his voice echoed between the two buildings in a way I can remember even to this day. There was the sound of the Custom House bell in Shanghai, for sure, with its repetition of bars from the *East is Red* song marking the hour. But behind this was the more consistent sound – of the whirring of boats as they went up and down the Huangpu River, a sign of constant industry, audible very clearly if you sat on outside terraces along the Bund, with the competing sounds of humans talking and shouting down on the waterfront below. In Hong Kong, there were boats too, boat horns sounding, and the ringing of the beeps as the Star Ferry closed and sent another service scuttling across the water to the other side. But here it was more often the wind, coming into the city and the great rising series of buildings, sometimes whistling between them, either a warning of a typhoon on its way, or simply the steady, gentle gusts on a reasonably windy day. In Xi'an, it was more the sound of people singing, like in Hohhot, either the karaoke classics from the partially opened doors of night-clubs I went by, or the rendition of the local folk music,

194 | EMPIRE OF THE SENSES

sometimes belted out by local performers or sung by people at parties, advertising that this place was, indeed, different.

Smells were easy to distinguish. The inimitable aroma of mutton boiling in large vats of water, with spring onion added, to make the most common banquet dish in Hohhot. Lamb meat seemed to have a thousand different smells there – some of them pungent like that of roasting, others mixed with the white spirit liquor they were often eaten with, and in the outer parts of the city, the smell of real lambs themselves, herded in to be sold at markets, or simply being transported from one grazing place to another. Xi'an was more about the spices that percolated through the air in the Muslim Quarter, the ways in which they assaulted the nostrils, some of them from chilli, cumin seeds, and the wonderful smell of different teas, coming either from sacks of goods outside ready to be sold, or escaping through the doors of small shops. In Beijing, it was the duck smell, in the small Li Qun Roast Duck Restaurant, a place that had been in business so long that the duck seemed to have soaked through to even the tables and the chairs and the wood on the walls, and the place was as much about that smell as the food it actually sold. Hong Kong was the same – smells that came from the many different kinds of food, or from markets selling different meats, fish or vegetables, some of them along tiny backstreets. Here the smell was all-pervasive, a kind of autocracy, powerful and pungent, an indivisible part of the city itself. Shanghai, for some reason, was the smells that existed in hotels, sometimes of flowers, or scents, something soothing and welcoming, that immediately marked their space of from the world outside.

Taste was about food – the foods from the times in China I had most enjoyed and made part of my staple. In Hohhot, it was the dumplings, and the way they comforted and stimulated because of their dependability and solidity, especially if they had been made during a party, with friends, or hosts. In Shanghai, it was fish, and the way that fish appeared in either Japanese food served there, as sashimi, with its smooth texture, or as part of a meal cooked in the Sichuanese style, hot with chilli, white and flaky, balanced by consumption alongside white rice. Xi'an was proud of is cuisine – its noodles. But for me, the most distinctive thing I had there was always the dumplings made in the Muslim Quarter, and the way that in the chilli sauce they became fiery and almost swallowed themselves into your stomach. In Hong Kong, despite all the amazing local food, and the international fair, some of it the most sophisticated in the world, it was the noodles sold in black liquid along one of the steep rising backstreets that most appealed – again because in eating something that seemed so simple, you were able to balance different flavours and sensations in one moment.

For feel, for how China touched and physically impacted, it was either the feel of the cold during the winter months in Hohhot, a touch that was like an icy hand, unmistakable and inimitable; or the water in the pools in Hong Kong, as I plunged into them from the hot world above, and momentarily felt their iciness before my body acclimatised. In Shanghai, it was the gusts of wind as they came, surprisingly, suddenly, from off the water, hitting me gently in the face, always welcome, always cooling, during the day or night, as I looked across to Pudong. In Xi'an, it was the feel of ancient buildings, running hands along the outside of the great walls of the old pagoda, imagining the memories carried in the bricks themselves, and the worlds they came from. Touching these places was a moment of connection, as was feeling the sculpted stone figures, the lions, with their smooth noses that stood in front of the Hong Kong and Shanghai Bank building along the Bund. In Beijing, it was the bark of trees that stood in the parks, places to rest when it was hot, to lean against, and recuperate.

China is written of as a place of history, culture, society and politics. Of course, it is all of these things. But this book has been about the specific place I have known, and which may exist perhaps only for me. But I offer it as an account of that encounter, of how the reality of one very different culture can have resonance and meaning to someone from somewhere very different. In the coming years, everyone will have a choice. To keep things that are different and alien to them at a distance, and to objectify and withhold from them, or to allow them access to their own inner lives, and to work through the complexities of what that means, and where it may end. That will not be an easy process, I know. It may well be very disruptive. But as this book shows, it is also something that can transform and enrich. And for that, I will always be grateful for the second life that experiencing, understanding and making life in China gave me. And I hope there will be many others who will journey along that same immensely rewarding route.

Kerry Brown
Canterbury, Kent
July 2018

NOTES

INTRODUCTION

1. FR Leavis, *Nor Shall My Sword: Discourses on Pluralism, Compassion and Social Hope*, Chatto and Windus, London, 1971.
2. During her visit to China in the 1960s, for instance, French philosopher Simone de Beauvoir changed planes five times. That was standard for this era.
3. Traditional characters (*fantizi*) are the full form written Chinese that appeared in texts through the classical era. Simplified characters (*jiantizi*) were created as part of a movement from the early twentieth century to reform language and spread literacy, making written Chinese easier to learn.
4. Nicholas Howe, *Writing the Map of Anglo-Saxon England: Essays in Cultural Geography*, Yale University Press, Yale, 2008, p.147.
5. Michel de Certeau, *The Practice of Everyday Life*, translated by Steven F Rendall, University of California Press, Berkeley and London, 1984.
6. David Bonavia, *The Chinese* (revised edition), Penguin Group, USA, 1989.

HOHHOT

1. Caroline Alexander, *The Way to Xanadu*, Weidenfield and Nicholson, London, 1993.
2. In 2012, it was accorded the status of a World Heritage site.
3. Standard Mandarin is in four tones for each syllable – a rising, falling, flat and then rising and falling combined tone. The syllable 'ma' therefore, depending on the tone, can mean either a horse, or cursing someone.
4. Jon Savage, *England's Dreaming: The Sex Pistols and Punk Rock*, Faber and Faber, London, 1991.
5. See N Kershaw, 'The Ruin' in *Anglo-Saxon and Norse Poems*, Cambridge University Press, Cambridge, 1922.

BEIJING

1. For a wonderful description of this process, and of how pretty much any part of the British landscape is the result of human intervention, see the great natural historian, Oliver Rackham, *Woodlands*, Collins, London, 2010.

2. See Edgar Snow, *Red China Today: The Other Side of the River*, Random House, New York, 1962.

3. See Aeneas Anderson, *A Narrative of the British Embassy to China in the Years 1792, 1793, and 1794 – Containing the Various Circumstances of the Embassy, with Accounts of the Customs and Manners of the Chinese, and Description of the Country Towns, Cities, etc.*, J. Debrett, London, 1796.

4. Francois Jullien, *A Treatise on Efficacy: Between Western and Chinese Thinking*, translated by Janet Lloyd, University of Hawaii Press, Honolulu, 2004, p.1.

5. Ibid, p.15.

6. Edward Said, *Orientalism: Western Conceptions of the Orient*, Pantheon Books, New York, 1978.

7. Donald J Munro, *The Concept of Man in Early China* (revised edition), University of Michigan Press, Ann Arbor, 2001, p. 1.

8. Ibid, p.49. See also Donald J Munro, *The Concept of Man in Contemporary China*, University of Michigan Press, Ann Arbor, 1977.

9. This place had been one of the most frequently used by the first American representative to the People's Republic of China, David Bruce, during his tenure in the city from 1973 to 1974. See David Bruce, *Window on the Forbidden City: The Beijing Diaries of David Bruce, 1973-1974*, edited by Priscilla Roberts, Hong Kong University Press, Hong Kong, 2001.

SHANGHAI

1. Andrew Field, *Shanghai's Dancing World: Cabaret Culture and Urban Politics, 1919-1954*, Columbia University Press, New York, 2011.

2. Jeffrey Wasserstrom, *Global Shanghai: 1850-2010: A History in Fragments*, Routledge, London, 2009.

3. Yasheng Huang, *Capitalism with Chinese Characteristics*, Cambridge University Press, Cambridge, 2008.

4. Fei, Xiaotong, *From the Soil: The Foundations of Chinese Society*, translated by Gart G Hamilton and Wang Zheng, University of California Press, Berkeley, CA, 1992.

XI'AN

1. There has been an excellent scholarly work that has compared the two eras, edited by German sinologist Walter Scheidel, *Rome and China: Comparative Perspectives on Ancient World Empires*, Oxford University Press, Oxford, 2009.
2. Mark Edward Lewis, *China's Cosmopolitan Empire: The Tang Dynasty*, Balknap Press, Harvard, Cambridge Mass, 2009.
3. Edward Gibbon, *Decline and Fall of the Roman Empire*, Penguin Edition, London, in three volumes, 2000.
4. Gildas, *On the Ruin of Britain* (translation from the Latin), Serenity Publishers, LLC, 2009. See also the wonderful description of this period in Robin Fleming, *Britain After Rome: The Fall and Rise 400-1070*, Penguin, London, 2011.
5. AW Clapham, *English Romanesque Architecture Before the Conquest*, Clarendon Press, Oxford, 1930, p.33.
6. See David Parsons and Diana Sutherland, *The Anglo-Saxon Church of All Saints, Brixworth, Northamptonshire: Survey, Excavation and Analysis, 1972-2010*, Oxbrow Books, Oxford, 2013.
7. Marcel Proust, *Against Sainte-Beuve and Other Essays*, translation by John Sturrock, Penguin, Harmondsworth, 1988, p.3.

HONG KONG

1. Jan Morris, *Hong Kong*, Random House, New York, 1989.
2. Niall Ferguson, *Empire: How Britain Made the Modern World*, Penguin Books, London, 2003, is the main statement of this line of argument by him.
3. See Christopher New, *A Change of Flags*, Bantam Books, London, 1990.
4. Kerry Brown, *Struggling Giant: China in the 21st Century*, Anthem Press, London and New York, 2007.
5. Leo F Goodstadt, *Poverty in the Midst of Affluence: How Hong Kong Mismanaged its Prosperity*, Hong Kong University Press, Hong Kong, 2013.

EMPIRE OF THE SENSES

1. Roland Barthes, *Empire of Signs*, translation by Richard Howard, Hill and Wang, New York, 1982.

ABOUT THE AUTHOR

Kerry Brown is professor of Chinese Studies and director of the Lau China Institute at King's College in London. He is an associate of the Asia Pacific Programme at Chatham House in London, an adjunct of the Australia New Zealand School of Government in Melbourne, and co-editor of the *Journal of Current Chinese Affairs*, run from the German Institute for Global Affairs in Hamburg. From 1998 to 2005, he worked at the British Foreign and Commonwealth Office as first secretary at the British Embassy in Beijing, and then as head of the Indonesia, Philippine and East Timor Section.

He has a Master of Arts from Cambridge University, a Postgraduate Diploma in Mandarin Chinese (distinction) from Thames Valley University, London, and a PhD in Chinese Politics and Language from Leeds University. He is the author of almost twenty books on modern Chinese politics, history and language, including *CEO, China: The Rise of Xi Jinping* and *China's World: What Does China Want?*

ABOUT ACA

We hope you enjoyed these insights into China at the turn of the 21st century.

ALAIN CHARLES ASIA publishes an exciting range of China-focused non-fiction. From the soaring highs and grim lows of China's tumultuous history to the vivid life stories of its major and minor players, ACA has books for anyone eager to learn more about this vast, diverse nation.

To let us know what you thought of this book, or to learn more about the eclectic selection of titles we offer, find us online. If you're as passionate about books as we are, then we'd love to hear your thoughts!

alaincharlesasia.com
@aca_pub